A Word for Your Year
Forty Assembly Kits
for the Secondary School Year

A Word for Your Year

Forty Assembly Kits
for the Secondary School Year

Dee Moss

Illustrated by Michael Moss

Collins

Collins Liturgical Publications
8 Grafton Street, London W1X 3LA

Distributed in Ireland by
Educational Company of Ireland
21 Talbot Sreet, Dublin 1

Collins Liturgical Australia
PO Box 3023, Sydney 2001

ISBN 0 00 599840 9
© 1986 Dee Moss
First published 1986

Typographical design by Colin Reed
Typesetting by John Swain & Son

Printed in Great Britain
by Bell and Bain Ltd, Glasgow

Contents

Key A Anytime themes   R Religious themes   S School-related themes   T Topical themes

Booklists and Indexes

Dedication and Acknowledgements

A Word For Your Year is dedicated to the pupils of King Charles the First School, Kidderminster. They said to me so often, 'Help . . . it's my turn to take assembly', that I realised the need to collect ideas and provide help in translating them into practical assemblies that young people could cope with on their own.

My thanks also go to the many individuals and organisations who sent material to aid my search for information. Many have agreed to be approached by pupils working with this book. I have learned a great deal while doing the research for these assembly kits, — most of all, a deep respect for the work done by charity groups all over the country. If I have omitted any from the list on page 121, I hope they will forgive me.

Another unexpected bonus has been the new insights I have gained into the beliefs of people whose traditions are different from my own. The Wolverhampton Interfaith Centre was a mine of information and I pay tribute to Ivy Gutridge and Rev Indejit Bhogal, who kindly checked my script where it touched on their sphere of work. They introduced me to the helpful Kartar Surindar Singh. Celia Collinson was also generous with expertise in this field.

My special thanks for the use of their stories goes to Group Captain Leonard Cheshire VC OM DSO DFC; Lt Col Terry Crump, Superintendent, The Corps of Queen's Messengers; Sir Ranulph Fiennes DSO; Audrey Miller; Martin Palmer MA; Jimmy Savile OBE; Sir John Wilson CBE.

Many librarians helped me in my work — at The British Library, at Birmingham, Kidderminster, Oxford, and Wolverhampton Public Libraries; and especially Miss L. Hart, BA ALA, who prepared the sample bibliographical suggestions on page 119.

Many other people have proffered useful ideas, notably Frances Anderson and Ken Miles — and, of course, the pupils at my school who started me off on this quest. Many of the chapters are based on kits originally prepared for them in our school library.

Barbara Maiden typed my manuscript with speed and enthusiasm, and Sue Chapman has been a patient and inspirational editor.

Heartfelt thanks go to my husband, Michael, who during the nine months of gestation of this book has put up with much, with unfailing good humour and support.

Dee Moss

My turn to take assembly . . . help!

Introduction for pupils

Perhaps you have offered to lead the thinking for your house, your year, or even for the whole school. Maybe it was a case of 'You, Susan, and you, Simon, next Friday, please.' You can't argue with a teacher but you can plead for *time* . . . to do anything well in public takes time to think, plan, prepare.

First of all, forget that this is a chore. Decide to produce something that is not only meaningful but has some sparkle. It must be meaningful to you; be clear what your message is, and believe it. You know how quick you are to spot insincerity, how some assemblies are so lifeless you know the leader doesn't really care about the subject. So choose an idea that truly appeals to you and work to develop it in your own way. If claiming your rights is important to you, look at kit no. 8, Equality, or no. 11, Fair Trading. If you care about conservation, consider what you could do with Rubbish (no. 29). You will find a subject index on page 123.

Do you want to be topical? You may find that your assembly date falls near Barbed Wire Day (no. 3), or May Day (no. 22). Another way to focus on the events around you, and so make your assembly topical, is to consider the year from various aspects:

1. *The school year* has notable occasions — first days of term, sports days, prize-giving and so on. These are listed and linked in the subject index (p. 123).

2. There is *the religious year*, not exclusively Christian but, like Harvest (no. 14) and New Year (no. 36), celebrated at various times by people of different traditions of faith.

3. There are *truly topical events*, like general elections or mine disasters, which hit national headlines, and there are more immediate happenings, like the death of a teacher or pupil.

If there is no obviously topical link, look at the Anytime assemblies and choose one you care about and can adapt to your school's need.

Remember to enter the date and group, with your initials, in the Assembly Checklist columns on pp. 125 ff. This will prevent overlapping and repetition.

When you have decided on your theme, read the chapters which seem relevant and, if you can, talk them over with someone who is on your wavelength. *Be adventurous*, remember you are not tied to words alone. You could make a collage, act a role-play, introduce music and all kinds of audio-visual aids. Approach teachers for help — the music and art departments are the most likely, but there are usually all kinds of experience and talent among people in schools.

You will discover that most of these assembly kits suggest that you contact groups or individuals outside the school. Enquire whether there is a school fund which would pay for two-way postage: while all the organisations listed on page 121 have promised to respond to your requests, most require their postal costs in advance. I have been joyfully surprised by the willingness of so many people to help, to be involved in what you are doing for your school. Just remember to send really courteous, if informal, requests, and to write in good time.

"BE ADVENTUROUS"

If you have occasion to visit outside establishments, like the police station, the hospital, or a church or temple, remember you go in the name of your school and be specially careful about behaviour. Churches, synagogues and temples have codes of practice which could give offence if not observed, so make sure that you know what will be expected before you go.

One of the happiest things about preparing these kits has been the contact with famous people. It seemed right to include some people who have done important things and are still alive — so many books are about dead heroes! For me, learning about the lives and thoughts of Group-Captain Leonard Cheshire, Sir Ranulph Fiennes, Jimmy Savile and Sir John Wilson was fascinating . Their ready response for permission for you to quote them gave the assemblies a new dimension. All these people have made their mark on society in very individual ways.

A Word for Your Year is meant to give you the opportunity to do just that. To make your own mark on something which is very important, an act we all share at the start of some school days. As you read the kits, you will discover many options. If your school usually ends assemblies with a prayer, you will see that each kit has a conclusion which will readily adapt into a prayer.

Use all the opportunities available. Go to the school library and the public library if possible. Pick the librarians' brains — they are trained to help you find the information you want. Check with your teaching staff if you are going to be adventurous, and use their expertise whenever you can.

So when the word comes that a certain day will be your assembly, take the opportunity and make it really your own . . . a word for your year.

Introduction for teachers

Assemblies can present problems quite out of proportion to the time they occupy in a school week. This is not a book to help you prepare material — it is intended as an ideas-pack for pupils who have offered, or been detailed, to lead the assembly for their year or house. Inevitably, on a busy day, teachers send pupils to the library to find the information they need.

School and public librarians, who also have a thousand and one things to do, cannot always produce the ideas and topic material needed in the short time allowed. This book is intended as a guide to enable young people to focus on a theme related to the school year, the religious calendars or topical events. A few 'Anytime' suggestions are included for those days when there is no obvious peg on which to hang thoughts.

While I would not compromise my own Christian faith, I am aware that in many schools there are teachers and pupils from different traditions of faith, and some who prefer a secular assembly. The presentations given here are open-ended — just how the themes are developed is very flexible and will reflect the personal inclinations of the presenters.

Many of the ideas in these kits need investigation since my aim was not only to offer assembly themes but to encourage information-seeking and the proper use of libraries. Addresses are given of many groups and departments which have agreed to supply material and/or answers to pupils' questions. Since up to a month may elapse from the time the pupils contact the source to the receipt of a reply, it is essential that the pupils are warned in good time. At least a week will be needed to prepare the role plays and other active renderings of dramatic themes.

Students will need guidance about appealing to outside bodies for help; a sample letter may be useful. Please ensure that adequate postage is enclosed for replies unless otherwise stated in the text. If local bodies are approached it is as well to prime the pupils about the necessary courtesies. This particularly applies to religious groups: for example, the need to cover heads and feet when visiting some temples, no smoking in places of worship, and so on.

A word of advice about the reverence required when handling scriptures from various traditions of faith is advisable.

Co-operation throughout the school will achieve much: the librarian will need to be involved, and the member of staff responsible for audio-visual aids. The help of the art and music departments will be very useful also.

The assemblies have several aims. First to focus on the spiritual and material needs we have in today's world. Next, to be lively and interesting, involving as many people as possible in their preparation and presentation. Lastly, to sharpen the pupils' awareness of how to use reference material and the wealth of information available once they know where to look.

It is necessary to keep a record of the date each assembly is used and the group to whom it was presented. Otherwise, overlapping may occur. Since I give many options in each kit this would not be disastrous, but it is a problem easily avoided if a brief note is made in the Assembly Checklist columns on pp. 125 ff.

" TEACHERS AND LIBRARIANS
SHOULD BE FRIENDS "

Please check with your school librarian that basic reference books are in stock — the Booklist on page 113 gives a brief guide. If, however, your school library is the cupboard-in-the-corridor type, don't despair. Take, or send, your group to the public library or invite the librarian to visit you. To plagiarise Oklahoma, 'teachers and librarians should be friends'. Getting together on the Assembly Line could be beneficial to all.

1
Actions mean more than words
The Story of Kelly

Aim

To discover different ways of caring in the community.

Facts

● *Find out from books* In this case, maybe your local newspaper will be most useful. It probably has an office where you can read through recent copies to find stories of people helping others. For this assembly, don't look for routine examples of fund-raising, but seek practical ways in which somebody has really helped another person.

● *Find out from people* Ask an old person, or somebody who is disabled, very tactfully, if they are ever helped by other folk. Perhaps you could find out from them how they would like to be helped.

Readings

Many organisations, like the guides and scouts, have words about helping others. Alternatively, all religions have many great passages on this topic. Look at the books marked with an asterisk in the General Booklist at the back of this book.

Music

The song 'If I can help somebody' has good words, but you may know another song on this theme which is more modern. . . .

Presentation

If you have unearthed a really good story from the newspapers you have read, use this. It may be that some children have had a toy-sale to raise money for a charity, or children have taken a concert to an old folks' home. . . . We are looking for very practical ways to show we care.

In a small industrial town in the Midlands lives a family of five. Parents, two daughters, and a son. They were not rich but they were very happy, until it was found that the younger girl had a serious eye problem. When she was two, she lost the sight of one eye and after a year of hospital treatment, the family had to face the sad fact that their youngest member would soon be quite blind.

Desperately they tried to give little Kelly sights to remember — they took her to the seaside so that she'd know what a beach looked like, and they introduced her to animals so that she could picture a monkey and a horse. . . . In three short weeks the blow fell, and Kelly found herself in a dark world. Daytime was difficult, but for this very small girl the nights were worst of all. She was afraid to sleep alone, but her bedroom was too small for two beds and her parents couldn't afford to buy bunks.

So big sister Tracey offered to sleep on a sunbed in Kelly's room, to be near if the little girl was afraid. Sun-bed mattresses are fine for a night or two. They are not so good as a permanent bed, but eleven year old Tracey was determined to put up with the discomfort to help Kelly.

Then somebody else took a hand in the caring . . . the manager of a local furniture shop! He heard about the family's problems and asked his head office if he could give Kelly and Tracey bunk beds, so they could share a room in comfort. Permission was gladly given and soon the brand-new bunks arrived — with an extra gift, a huge cuddly bear for little Kelly.

Most of us find, as Kelly has done, that when troubles come our parents and brothers and sisters do all they can to help. It's also true that other people, even strangers, like the manager of that furniture shop, are willing to offer not just practical help, but the extra sparkle that can bring joy in sadness.

People often say the papers are full of nothing but trouble. The story of Kelly was front-page news in that Midlands town. Most places have similar heart-warming stories of caring if we look for them.

Perhaps we could do more than read about helping people in need? Maybe there's somebody in our town, perhaps even in our street, possibly in our very house, who needs help we can give?

Conclusion

There are so many ways to show we care. Nobody can be too young or too shy — everyone is needed!

2
Animals

This is an anytime assembly, but if there is local or national news featuring an animal, it could be topical. If you are asked to do an assembly near 17 March, remember that as well as being St Patrick's Day, this is also Noah's Ark Day and you may choose to use some of the ideas here to commemorate that.

Aim

To acknowledge the large part animals play in our lives, and to consider our responsibilities to them.

Music

There are so many pieces of music, from the Saint Saens 'Carnival of the Animals' to popular songs, that you have a wide choice of sounds to set your scene.

Props

Make a collage, with art department help if necessary, of animals. You may choose to depict them as wild and wonderful, domestic and appealing or, more shockingly, in captive or painful states. Leaflets and material from The Royal Society for the Prevention of Cruelty to Animals will make a good setting. Write to The Education Dept., RSPCA, Causeway, Horsham, W. Sussex RH12 1HG.

If you have school pets, or if you and your friends have the type of domestic animals which would be permitted in an assembly, they would add a very special dimension to your material.

Readings

There are many poems and passages of prose which say a great deal about animals. This is an occasion to let your personal feelings, and the aspect of animals you have decided to focus on, direct your choice.

Remember that most faiths have something to say about animals, and their views differ considerably, so you will need to be aware of the sensitivity of this subject and angle it not to give offence.

Facts

● *Find out from books* Most school libraries have shelves of books about animals; choose those which fit your theme.

The RSPCA (address above) has an education department which is extremely helpful. They will supply, at your request, a wealth of information and ideas. You could also contact your local branch to see if such material is available there.

● *Find out from people* Your nearest RSPCA inspector will probably have true and interesting stories to tell about incidents near your school. If he can't attend the assembly he will give you stories you can quote of animal rescue, and cases where the Society has prevented suffering.

Talk to people who rely on their animals, like blind men and women with their dogs, or a totter (rag and bone man) who still uses a horse for his business, or a shepherd who has a sheepdog. Farmers are a good source of information.

Visual Aids

The RSPCA leaflet, *Animal Welfare on Film*, lists fourteen films which are lent, free, to schools for occasions like assemblies. Remember that you need to cooperate with your visual aids department, and plan well ahead. Two or three weeks' notice is needed to obtain the film, and you must pay the postage both ways.

Presentation

Focus first on the part animals play in our lives, avoiding the meat aspect if you have non-meat eaters in your group.

You could speak of the pleasure of pets, of working animals like sheepdogs, or

CRUELTY TO GOLDFISH

quote some of the remarkable animals who have rescued people from danger. The files of old newspapers and many books reveal these. In Scotland, there is a monument to an Edinburgh dog called Greyfriars Bobby, a faithful companion who refused to leave his master's grave.

The bulk of your time will be spent on whichever aspect of the RSPCA's work you feel is important for your time and place. If there is a fairground locally where goldfish are given as prizes, you will find the leaflet on this very helpful.

Should you have Moslem or Jewish pupils in your school, you may find it useful to consider the leaflet on ritual slaughter, which explains the law on this subject, and its implications for the animals, very clearly.

Animal experiments are giving rise to much discussion, particularly in schools. The leaflet about this will give ammunition if you feel this is an unnecessary cruelty.

Hedgehogs, badgers, swans and many other creatures are in danger from people who would never knowingly hurt a living creature. Use the leaflets about them to show your group what they can do to prevent suffering.

You may decide to present your ideas in a dialogue form, with a friend, or to use several voices in a kind of shock tactic, with quieter explanations and suggestions of ways to help. This is a very evocative subject, and needs careful handling, but you'll find it will stimulate a lot of thought and discussion.

Conclusion

Imagine a world without cats and dogs, horses and sheep, birds and fish. Pause for a moment to consider the cruelty people inflict on creatures that can't defend themselves. Make up your mind today that no animal will ever suffer because of your lack of care.

3
Barbed Wire Day
Amnesty International

Aim

To focus on the political prisoners of the world, and be thankful for our freedom.

Music

You may be able to find an old recording of the song 'Don't Fence Me In' or perhaps you know something more modern about people in un-free situations.

Collage

Collect large pictures of faces. They may be cut from magazines or posters, but they must be varied . . . different colours, ages, types. When you have glued the cut-outs to a board, stretch pieces of barbed wire across the collage and carefully staple it in place. You will then have a group behind a barbed wire fence. . . .

Facts

● *Find out from books* Read an account of life as a political prisoner. Your school librarian will help you find what is in stock. Pastor Wurmbrand is a good name to look for. From the public library or your telephone book, find the address of Amnesty International's local group. Write to Amnesty International (AI) at 8 Southampton Street, London WC2E 7HF for information.

● *Find out from people* Ask your local Amnesty International if there is a special prisoner whom they try to help. Get details of this man or woman and use them as the focal point of your assembly — it will be much more moving if it has a really local link.

Presentation

News headlines could make this a topical occasion if a political prisoner is causing comment.

The week including 25 June could feature this theme as an anniversary, probably one which has never been featured in a school assembly before. Like most inventions, barbed wire seems such a simple idea, we wonder why it had never been made before. For many years strands of strong wire had been used to keep cattle in a field, but on 25 June, 1867, in Ohio, USA, the first patent for barbed wire was taken out. The strands of wire were cruelly spiked with metal points to deter any attempts to pass the fence. The invention worked, and farmers found it easier to control their animals.

Sadly, men found another use for barbed wire . . . it became an effective way to fence people in too! Today, all round the world, men, women and young people are imprisoned, not because they are criminals but because they have their own ideas which differ from the ideas of the rulers of their countries.

If you can obtain permission, you may find that a member of Amnesty International from your area will be happy to speak for a few minutes about the work of this organisation.

Otherwise, choose one of the many people featured in the AI literature and tell his or her story, and the efforts made to effect release.

Alternatively, you may like to imagine you are a prisoner of conscience and write a letter to be smuggled out and read to the assembly. It should tell your beliefs, explain how they differ from your government's and why you are prepared to suffer for the sake of ideals. It should also underline the longing for freedom — for your country to be free.

Finally, remind your hearers how much freedom we all enjoy and how greatly it should be treasured. Suppose, when you left school today, you found the gates barred by painful, spikey wire . . . be thankful that barbed wire day holds no terrors for us.

Conclusion

We all take freedom for granted, yet it is a most precious gift. Those of us who value our freedom should be aware of those who are fenced in for unjust reasons, and decide if we can help them.

4
Big happenings often have small beginnings
Leonard Cheshire VC, OM, DSO, DFC

Aim

To show that great good may grow from tiny acts of kindness. (If used on a remembrance occasion, this assembly may underline the importance of acts of love rather than acts of hate.)

Music

You may like to have a tape of the RAF march fading into your start. The Dam Busters March would also be appropriate.

Facts

● *Find out from books* Read *Cheshire VC* by Russell Braddon (Evans, 1965) or, better still, read his own book called *The Hidden World* (Collins).

● *Find out from people* Ask your older relations what they remember about Leonard Cheshire from wartime days. He had many decorations; what do they stand for? Find out! Discover if there is a Cheshire Home in your area. If so, try to visit it and talk with the staff and residents, especially the young ones.

Presentation

Particularly if this assembly is linked to a wartime memorial anniversary, you may like to explain the honours Leonard Cheshire won. Few people have a record of courage and leadership like his; but now the name of Cheshire reminds us of help for the suffering, not honours in battle.

Leonard Cheshire was a bomber pilot in the second world war. He became group captain with the famous 617 (Dam Busters) squadron and later was sent to observe the dropping of the atom bomb on Nagasaki in Japan.

The end of the war found him saddened by the suffering the war had caused and determined to find a way in which he and people like him could lead peaceful, useful lives. Cheshire thought that a group of people, living and working together in a community might be the answer, but in practice he found that such an enterprise was more difficult to get going than he had expected. Soon most of the people who had shared his vision and lived on his property had drifted off and he was left with a rambling, empty house — called Le Court — no money and no job. Leonard Cheshire desperately wanted to be useful, but he was determined to take no job that would be at the expense of another person.

Then he heard about Arthur, the pig-man. Arthur had looked after the pigs at Cheshire's commune but was now in hospital, suffering from incurable cancer. The hospital wanted his bed for someone with a chance of recovery . . . because there was no place in those days for incurables. Arthur's situation was desperate. Leonard had a huge, empty house. Almost on impulse, he offered Arthur a home at Le Court, and within days the former bomber pilot had become a kind of nurse.

Before he died, Arthur spoke of the future of Le Court. He foresaw that the twenty-five bedrooms could be usefully filled with folk like himself, sick and with nowhere to live. He begged Leonard Cheshire that if anyone else like himself arrived, he would not be turned away.

It was not a 'he' but a 'she' who came next! An old lady of ninety-one came in an ambulance, wearing a hat with long feathers that nodded in time with the stretcher-bearers' steps. This was Granny, a great character who gave Cheshire many trials and also much love. . . .

Within months there were thirty invalids living at Le Court. Soon other Cheshire homes were opened round Britain. It was not as easy as it sounds. Leonard Cheshire became very ill himself and had many operations. Money had to be raised to build and maintain the Homes. Committees were formed and the work spread overseas. Today, there are 75 Cheshire Homes in Great Britain and 146 world-wide, some devoted entirely to the needs of disabled young people.

Leonard Cheshire had two great strengths . . . a real faith, which began as a spark caught from the dying pig-man, and a wonderful wife, Sue, who shared his vision of help for a suffering world.

If it helps your assembly, you may quote a few words Leonard Cheshire wrote to me when he was asked if he might be featured in this book: 'Of course, there are two sides to achieving peace on earth. There is peace-keeping (the role of the policeman) and peace-building, which involves doing everything in our power to strike at the roots of confrontation and war, and particularly working to remove injustice and to help the poorer nations of the world onto their feet economically.'

Nobody, least of all Leonard Cheshire could have suspected, when he took one cancer victim into his home, that from this simple act of kindness a world-wide community offering comfort and hope would grow. Think about this, next time you're asked to give a hand.

Conclusion

We are often put off doing something to help other people because our own views are too narrow. We think we are too young, too ordinary or just too limited to help all the suffering in the world. The problem is too big, so we do nothing.

5

Death —
The Final Adventure

Jimmy Savile, OBE

Aim

To think about death, through the eyes of someone who sees it at close hand.

Readings

There are many poems about death. A book by poets of the world wars may be your key, but talk to your school or public librarian about poetry on this theme.

Facts

● *Find out from books* Read all you can about the beliefs of different faiths on this subject. F.G. Herod, *What Men Believe* has a good survey (Methuen Educational Ltd, 1980); C. Collinson and C. Miller, *Milestones* (E. Arnold, 1984) is excellent, so is *Death* in the Living Faiths series, edited by J. Prickett, (Lutterworth, 1980) which has many quotes. K. Milne, *A Time to Die* (Wayland, 1977) is thought-provoking.

If you can find a copy of Jimmy Savile's little book, *God'll Fix It* (Mowbray, 1979) you will find it revealing and helpful.

● *Find out from people* Talk with people of various beliefs in your school, or your street, about their views on death — tactfully!

Presentation

Probably the hardest thing most of us will have to face in our lives is the death of someone we love dearly. Perhaps this has already happened to you; indeed you may have chosen this assembly because a teacher or pupil in your school has died.

Death leaves us with a sense of loss, and many questions which have few clear answers. Some people, like Christians, who have a real trust in the after-life, think of death as the start of a richer and more wonderful existence.

Others, like Hindus and Buddhists, believe that they are part of a cycle of life and death, returning to the world in different forms, according to how they have behaved before.

Shintoists have little interest in life after death, because they believe supremely in the importance of this life. Sikhs feel that reincarnation will continue until perfect human life earns them life with God.

Jews feel that the soul is immortal and they still wait for the coming of their Messiah, when the dead will rise. Many see death as a temporary separation, and believe that a reunion will attend the Day of Judgment. With so many beliefs, unless one has a very sure faith it is no wonder that death seems perplexing and frightening.

Jimmy Savile, the TV personality and disc jockey, has a deep Christian faith but is honest enough to admit to many doubts and questions. Although he is so famous, rich and popular, Jimmy spends much of his spare time as a voluntary worker in a hospital. Sometimes his duties as a porter mean that he has to take the bodies of people who have died to the mortuary where they are prepared for the funeral.

Many of these people were known to him before they died and some have discussed death with him. His conclusion, which he tries to share with them, is obvious yet rather startling. The obvious bit is that death is inevitable ... inescapable. In his book, *God'll Fix It*, Jimmy explains that just as we have all been born, so one day we shall die. His reaction to the obvious is that death is the last great adventure. He writes that he looks forward to it with considerable excitement! Jimmy believes that after his death he will again meet his mother, whom he calls the Duchess, and all the other people he has loved in life.

He honestly feels that the Duchess is with him now, closer than when she was alive, and he comforts grieving relatives with this thought. Jimmy Savile's faith gives him comfort in the present and confidence for the future. It is shared, in different ways, by many people who trust God not just for this life but for the great adventure of death.

A schoolgirl, on her first holiday abroad, was terrified of the mountain chair-lifts in Austria, though most of the party were thrilled to be launched in a frail-looking seat and whisked high above the valley, suspended by a metal hook. At last the girl was persuaded to let herself be carried up the mountain, but her pleasure in the magnificent view was spoiled by her fear of getting off the chair, which she knew would not stop for her to alight at the top.

In fact, as the gleaming summit of the mountain came into view, she saw a large, smiling man on the platform. As she undid the chain which had kept her in the seat, a strong arm reached out and a firm hand pulled her to safety. Perhaps this parable, or story, illustrates Jimmy Savile's belief that death is the last great adventure.

Conclusion

Death is the one certainty for us all. Its time and its manner are unknown, but we must all die. For many people death is the last great adventure.

6
Easter

Aim

To look at why we have Easter Eggs.

Props

Collect different signs of Easter-time. Spring flowers. Fluffy chicks. (If you live in the country, you may be able to bring a few live chicks to school. If not, buy two or three decoration chicks from a cake-decorating shop.) Chocolate eggs, and some you have decorated yourselves, using blown eggs: your art teacher may help you with the decorations. A glass tumbler. A blown egg.

● *To blow an egg*
Make small holes in each end of an egg and cover them with sticky tape. Then push a needle gently round until the hole is large enough to blow through. Use a long thin needle to break the yolk, then hold the egg over a cup and blow gently until the contents of the egg are in the cup. Run water in one hole and blow it out the other until it runs clear.

Facts

● *Find out from books* Look up all you can discover about Easter games. Many books give details about Easter celebrations in various countries. (B. Scholfield, *Events in Britain*, Blandford Press, is excellent for British customs.)

● *Find out from people* Ask old people and local historians if there has ever been an egg-rolling, or other Easter customs, in your area.

Readings

The New Testament story of the empty tomb (Mark 16, verses 1-11) may be read in a modern version.

Music

A good modern Easter hymn may be chosen — 'Christ the Lord is risen today' or 'Thine be the glory, risen conquering Son': to be sung by all, or listened to on a record.

If you want a non-religious piece, choose something like the song 'Easter Parade'. The aria 'Rejoice for the Lord has arisen' from the opera *Cavalleria Rusticana* is suitable.

Presentation

This is the last assembly before you break up for Easter . . . great! One of the best things about Easter is that you get — days off school. But it's not like Christmas — in

December before you break up there are carols and Christmas trees, cards and gifts — everyone knows what Christmas is for.

Easter is less obvious, but there are still a few signs of what it's all about. Flowers, after the long dull winter. Chicks, and all the other signs of new life. For many of us there'll be an Easter egg or two, probably made of chocolate.

Eggs have been a sign of new life for thousands of years, in many parts of the world. People in China, Egypt, Greece and Persia used eggs as a sign of new life at their great spring festivals, long before Christians celebrated Easter. The Chinese were giving bright red eggs to their friends nine hundred years before the birth of Christ, because they saw them as a sign of life.

In Britain, America and Switzerland some people still play a game called egg-rolling, which has been known for generations. The eggs were hard-boiled, then coloured, or just marked with the player's name. A hill with a gentle slope was chosen and all the children and young people stood on the top with their eggs. At a given signal the eggs were sent rolling down the hill and the winner was the player whose egg rolled the farthest.

Easter eggs are fun, just because it's a fine excuse to enjoy chocolate or to chase coloured eggs down a hill, but for Christians the empty egg has a very special meaning. On the first Good Friday there were many grieving friends of Jesus who had seen him die on a cross. True, he had told them that death would not mean the end of all their hopes, promised that he would rise from the tomb, but how could they believe such a thing?

So, on the Sunday morning, a few of his closest friends went to his tomb — and found it empty! In the next forty days many of his friends saw him, walked, talked and ate with him, and they were all convinced: Jesus was alive, he had risen from the grave!

For Christians the egg became a sign of that empty tomb. Everyone knows that an egg is full. We break eggs into pans to fry for breakfast. We crack them over a bowl, and pour out the yolk and white to make a cake. Just like this! (Hold up your empty blown egg, then bang it hard on the rim of the glass tumbler as if the contents were going to spill into it. Of course, nothing will come out, so you can hold up the two empty halves of shell, for all to see.)

All round the world this Easter people will be celebrating, with great joy, the miracle of the empty tomb, which was Christ's answer to his enemies. It fulfilled his promise that he would be seen alive after death, and because that promise was kept, people who love him believe his other words . . . that he would always be with them and that after death, they would share his new life.

Conclusion

Symbols need to be meaningful. For many people the empty tomb is a sign of hope.

7
The empty envelope

Aim

To consider the opportunities and challenges offered by a new day/term/year.

Props

You will need ten envelopes, which look as if they've been through the post, with appropriate material inside. Prime ten pupils (teachers may be included if they agree) to read the contents of their numbered envelopes in sequence. The following are only suggestions — you may include anything which is meaningful to you.

Presentation

You will need a leader, to introduce the topic and to maintain the flow of envelope-opening. Make sure everyone can hear the readers . . . it may be best to ask them to come to the front . . . it's hard to hear through the back of someone's head!

Leader As we start a new day/week/term/year we each face an empty envelope. What's an envelope anyway? (Open a large plain envelope so that it appears as a shaped piece of paper.) Not a lot . . . but folded and glued it becomes a very important container to carry messages across town, across the world. What kind of envelopes have reached our doormats recently? What do their contents mean to us?

(Leader calls envelopes by number and their holders disclose the contents and read the messages.)

1. A letter . . . news from a friend, about school holidays/trips. (Add whatever is topical.)

Leader Mention news briefly . . . it's good to have friends, great to keep contact.

2. A bill . . . for goods bought.

Leader Tough, when money's short, but I've had the goods and I must pay what's due . . . bills must be paid.

3. Information . . . with a map. (Obtain a map from an estate agent's office. Read any notes about schools, churches, etc.)

Leader Great, now I won't be lost! It will be easy to find the hospital to visit a friend, to know where the park and the station are.

4. Love letter (Read suitable passage!)

Leader We all need to know we're loved, so it makes sense that we also need to say 'I love you'. Not just to girlfriends or boyfriends but to parents and others who may sometimes need to hear this said.

5. Careers pamphlet (police, nursing, whatever. . . . Read a little about qualifications needed and opportunities in work.)

Leader Most of us need info like this. We can reject it, say it's not for us, but there are always some opportunities we can take if we choose.

6. Appeal (your choice — Oxfam, Save the Children Fund, Shelter. . . . Read a few lines of the special needs, and the cash required to help.)

Leader We could put this one in the bin, too. But many families live on what we spend on a magazine, or makeup, or the scooter. . . . Makes you think doesn't it?

7. Birthday card with a £5 note from Uncle. (Read the words on the card.)

Leader Nice to be remembered. Birthdays are special, even for people our age. But they bring new responsibilities. Money's one. Uncle worked hard for that fiver. . . . I need to spend it carefully — and not to forget to send a thankyou!

8. Invitation (to a disco, party, whatever. . . . Read out details.)

Leader Good! We all need to unwind, to have fun with our friends. Music, dancing, sport . . . all part of the package in a day, a week, a year.

9. Official brown envelope — a demand — (a licence needed for TV . . . a scooter).

Leader No choice about this one . . . it's a demand. There are some things that have to be done, and we may as well do them quickly and cheerfully.

10. Free offer (Reader's Digest type if possible . . .). Just say yes or no to this tempting advertisement.

Leader But do we really want it? Do we ever get something for nothing? Decisions . . . decisions. . . .

Summary

Leader So . . . ten envelopes . . . each with something different, some good, some bad . . . like each day, week, term, year. Today's envelopes will hold demands to be met, choices to make, offers to accept or reject and love to give and receive. We have to sort out the good from the bad, help somebody if we can, share a bit of love, find time to work and play. And in the end, all that has been folded into this day will be over . . . tomorrow is another day!

Conclusion

No day/term/year is empty . . . it holds many different offers and tasks. Decisions have to be made, opportunities taken.

8
Equality

This will be topical if used around 21 March or 22 September. These are the equinox times when, twice a year, the whole world shares equal hours of daylight.

Aim

Using the equality of light as a 'peg', we look at racial equality. We consider Martin Luther King's example as a fighter for the rights of all people to be equal under the law.

Facts

● *Find out from books* Write to the Commission for Racial Equality for their leaflets. You will find a great deal of useful information in the material they produce.

Read a life of Martin Luther King: a good one is by Nigel Richardson in the Profiles Series, published by Hamish Hamilton in 1983. If time is short, look in a reference book under King for details of his life. Best of all, read Dr King's book of sermons, called *Strength to Love*, published by Collins Fontana in 1963.

● *Find out from people* If you have friends from different cultural backgrounds, ask if they feel they all have equal opportunities in every part of their lives. This assembly will be most effective if you have pupils of various racial origins.

Music

You may be able to play tapes, or even have live music which derives from different parts of the world.

Preparation

Today we celebrate the *Spring* (in March) or *Autumn* (in September) Equinox. Only twice each year does every country in the world have an identical number of daylight hours. True, the twilight may be shorter or longer, but the actual length of time when the sun's rays hit the earth is the same only at Equinox.

Think about the inequality of most things in the world. Some countries are rich, some are poor. Some people are free, others live in fear. Many people are hungry while others eat too much.

Something to celebrate then, in just this one thing we all have in common this week . . . twenty-four hours of equal light and darkness!

In every generation there have been men and women who have striven for equality, and many have died for this ideal. Others have given their thoughts, their prayers and their efforts to live for the dream that everyone should have equal opportunities.

If you have done your own research, talk about the life of Martin Luther King, quoting from his own words where possible. Use what follows only if you have no opportunity to research the life of Martin Luther King for yourself. Your own reactions and ideas are better than any material prepared for you.

What does it take to make you really angry? Probably many things, but it's likely that injustice would come high on your list. Mike King felt like that, as a teenager. His real name was Martin Luther King, but his family called him Mike, or M.L. . . .

Mike, like many teenagers, objected to his family's plans for him. When his father, who was a Baptist minister, hoped that his son would follow him into the church, Mike decided that he'd rather be a doctor or a lawyer. Later, when Mike fell in love with a lovely singer, his father felt she was not the right wife for him, but Mike married her just the same and never regretted his decision.

Many young men and women rebel against parental advice, and they don't make news, so what's special about Mike King? His anger against injustice, his deep belief in the equality of all people led him from the pulpit to street demonstrations, from the streets to the prison and from prison to the Nobel Prize for Peace. His actions gained him a place in the world's history books, and death by an assassin's bullet. Most important of all, his zeal meant that millions of black people, like him, received their rights . . . ending the indignities which began in slavery and persisted in freedom.

The descendants of the slaves in the Southern part of North America had been deprived and discriminated against for generations. Although they were not slaves anymore, but supposedly free men and women, their rights were curtailed so that, for example, they were not allowed to marry white partners, give evidence in trials of white people or even sit with whites in buses or trains.

A secret society, the Ku Klux Klan, fomented hatred against the black people and sometimes injured or killed them. As Mike King grew up, he began to feel that black people like himself should be equal in every way with the other citizens of America. Yet he would probably have remained the Baptist preacher he finally decided to be, if a black woman — Rosa Parks — in Montgomery where he lived with his wife, Coretta, and their baby, had not been arrested. Rosa Parks' crime was that she refused to give up her seat on a bus for a white person. When Rosa was taken to a police station and fingerprinted, indignation swept over the black population.

They were led, reluctantly at first, by Mike King, who decided that any protest must be peaceful. Although he was a fine wrestler, the young minister had no time for violent action. He was deeply influenced not only by Jesus Christ, but also by Ghandi, the Indian leader who had accomplished so much by peaceful protest. Forty thousand leaflets were distributed, asking blacks to refuse to travel in the segregated buses. Black taxi owners offered to charge passengers only the bus fare so that people could manage to get to work, though some had to walk or cycle long distances. On the first day of the action, only about twelve blacks used the hated buses. That night, at a great meeting, Mike urged the people to continue their non-violent protest with dignity and love. Nobody thought the blacks could keep their boycott up for very long, especially when a hate campaign began to terrorise the leaders. When Mike barely infringed a speed limit, he was put in prison. His home was bombed and his supporters were tempted to oppose violence with violence. Dr King urged them instead to love their enemies, to tread the path of peace.

After a year, the boycott ended because the American courts had declared that segregation on public transport was illegal, but Mike's fight against injustice had just begun. Now an acknowledged leader of the ill-treated black people, he spent the next years leading the fight for racial equality. As his cause scored more and more victories he was invited to Norway to receive one of the world's most honoured awards, the Nobel Peace Prize. He gave the money to the freedom movement, but an even greater achievement was waiting for him.

Later that year, 1964, he went to the White House to watch the President sign the Civil Rights Act. At last his dreams were coming true . . . equality was becoming a reality!

Mike King was not only a man of action . . . his gift for words is crystallised in his great 'dream' speech — given the day before his death — when he spoke of his vision that all God's children would one day join hands to sing 'Free at last. Great God Almighty, I'm free at last!'

Like Jesus Christ and Mahatma Gandhi, Martin Luther King met a violent death — he was shot by a white man.

Conclusion

As the Equinox reminded us, very few things in our world are equal, but when people care enough, and are prepared to make sacrifices for their ideals, equality can be achieved. Racial equality is spreading round the world, with a growing momentum. Let us be always vigilant to protect everyone's equality and to remember that the colour of our skin matters much less than the way we live our lives.

9
Every badge has something to say . . .

You may wish to tie this assembly to a school event, when the school badge will be much in evidence. On the other hand, this could be a topical assembly, using a parliamentary election or cup final to demonstrate the use of badges. It could also be an anytime assembly, demonstrating how many of us wear badges and the meaning behind some of them.

Aim

To take a look at the badges we wear.

Props

Either collect as many badges as you can, and wear them for the assembly, or make large copies of a few for display: feature your school badge, and vary the subject of the others as much as possible.

Music

A song about sharing would be appropriate if you use the story with this assembly.

Facts

● *Find out from books* You may discover that a history of your school or the story of its founding will explain the school badge: your school librarian will help you to research this. Other reference books will explain the meaning behind some other badges.

● *Find out from people* Ask anyone you see wearing an unusual badge what it means. Talk with Sikhs about the 'Khanda', their special emblem. Ask Christians why some of them wear a cross.

Presentation

Explain what you have discovered about badges in your own words. Many school badges have an interesting and pictorial history. Others like the tiny silkworm badge worn by many airmen during the second world war, commemorate an unusual fact: this person's life has been saved by a parachute. The silkworm badge honours the tiny creature which spun the material from which the parachutes were made. The airman's life hangs on the silken thread.

At election times many of us wear badges that show which party we favour — we are making a public statement of our preference for one political group. Most badges are like this . . . they tell the world what we believe.

You may want to speak about the pride of wearing a school badge, or one which shows you are a house captain or in a football team, or serve as a school librarian.

Perhaps you may wish to speak about the way badges are often ignored by other people, so that the statement made by wearing them is lost. If you are short on ideas, use the following story — which is a true one.

EVERY BADGE HAS SOMETHING
TO SAY

Mrs Smith had been staying with friends who lived a hundred and fifty miles from her home. At the end of her visit she'd been given sandwiches for her lunch, and the student son of the house offered to see her onto her train. As they said goodbye on the platform Glenn reached into his pockets and offered a handful of badges.

'Choose one' he said 'Most of them are from the Friends of the Earth.' Although Mrs Smith was not the kind of person who usually wore a badge, she took the largest and pinned it onto her coat. It was just four printed words: FOOD IS FOR SHARING.

In the bustle of finding a seat on a crowded train, thanking Glenn for his company and waving goodbye, Mrs Smith completely forgot that she was still wearing her badge. As the train sped North she was soon reading a magazine and she didn't feel hungry until the man who had been sitting opposite her went to the restaurant coach. He returned with a cup of coffee and a packet of crisps, which he began to eat.

Then Mrs Smith realised that the man was staring at her or, rather, at her coat. As the words on the label . . . FOOD IS FOR SHARING, battered his brain, he pushed the crisps towards Mrs Smith, who accepted several. Suddenly hungry, Mrs Smith opened the sandwiches she'd been given, and offered one to the stranger opposite. Across the train's aisle, some students returning to university watched the food-share and dug into their own luggage.

Soon pieces of chocolate, fruit, nuts, slices of cake were being handed round the whole compartment. Everyone was eating someone else's lunch, everyone was talking and laughing. The sedate quiet of the train journey was transformed into something very much like a party.

All because one man read a stranger's badge, and took it seriously. Life could be much better for many of us if badges were not just ornaments but a way of spreading good ideas.

Conclusion

We wear badges because we want to make a statement. Does what we say through our badges have an effect on our lives? Do they prompt a reaction from other people?

10
Everybody needs someone
The Samaritans

Aim

To feature everyone's need for understanding and advice.

Props

A phone. You can use a toy . . . or bring a real one. A phone directory.

Facts

● *Find out from books* Statistics on suicide (see Annual Abstracts of Statistics, Central Statistical Office, available in most reference libraries).

● *Find out from people* Look up the Samaritans in your local phone book. Ask to talk to somebody there about your topic. Write to The Samaritans Inc., 17 Uxbridge Road, Slough SL1 1SN.

Readings

Choose a passage from the Samaritans' literature, about the founding of the movement or about its work.

Music

Many popular songs are about despair . . . people leaving home, or feeling unloved. You may like to play a little of one of these.

Presentation

Everybody needs help sometimes. Usually we turn to our parents or friends, to doctors or teachers or the leaders of our faith. But there are times when it's easier to talk with a stranger, to listen to somebody with no connection to our problem.

The Samaritans is an organisation which exists to help people, particularly those who are so desperate that even life seems not worth having. You can locate the nearest branch from your phone book, and this may be the best way to find the facts you need. If you send a stamp to the head office listed above, you'll receive some excellent leaflets including a worksheet on How To Do a Project on the Samaritans.

If your research time is really short, and you cannot produce your own material in time, you could use three people to tell the following case studies, which have been approved by The Samaritans. Let your 'actors' tell these stories as if they had happened to them. You can make the characters any nationality to fit with people taking part in your assembly.

Martin

Martin had lived in a children's home for as long as he could remember. Some of the kids hated it and longed for the day when one or both of their parents would take them home. Others, like Martin, had no family, and day-dreamed that somebody would adopt them or at least take them to be fostered.

This seemed odd to Martin — he liked the Home. True, there were a lot of staff changes and it always unsettled him when a new Housemother and Father took charge of the group that Martin thought of as his family. But as he'd grown older he'd been given new responsibilities and he enjoyed playing big brother to the smaller ones.

He also liked the garden at the Home and loved having his own rabbit and a plot where he grew his favourite vegetable — sweetcorn. Every day he went to the nearby comprehensive school and he assumed that life would go on like this until he was eighteen, when he hoped to go to college.

Then, suddenly, all the children who were old enough to understand were told that the Home was to be closed. The young ones would be found foster-homes or sent to a smaller unit in another town. Others, like Martin, who were really old enough to leave school would be found lodgings, if they had no family to take them.

Martin was desperate. If he had to leave the Home, he wanted to live in a flat or house with the other teenagers and perhaps a Houseparent to help them. In this way he could finish his schooling with his friends and begin to live an adult life. The trouble was that nobody would listen to him. He felt he had no power to influence his own future. Nobody cared.

Somebody at school suggested that he should ring the Samaritans. He did so and then he visited their Centre. When all the options, as Martin saw them, had been talked through, he decided to write to a local councillor, explaining his problem. Eventually Martin's dream came true. He now shares a house, with three teenagers from the Home and an older couple who are not so much house-parents as friends.

Lin

Lin's parents ran a Chinese restaurant, so they were always busy. Not that Lin was lonely — you can't be lonely when you have a twin brother, and Lin had Philip. In a way, that was Lin's trouble, because he desperately wanted to be himself and everyone treated Lin and Phil as if they were one person. School uniform didn't help because it emphasised that they were look-alikes and though they had enjoyed teasing people about their identities when they were young, the joke faded at secondary school.

Lin wasn't jealous of Phil — he liked him too much for that, but Phil always had the edge — Lin could never beat him at anything. Worst of all was the attitude of the other pupils who were always saying things like 'It makes no difference that you are twins. If we had twenty Chinese at school, they'd all look the same to us.'

Night after night, Lin lay awake, longing to be himself, wanting to be somebody special. It seemed this would never happen. He pleaded with his parents to move to a Chinese community where there would be more young people like himself, but their work was in the town and they had a good business. They couldn't even see that a move to a different school would help Lin — it made sense to them that twins should stay together. Somehow nobody understood Lin's need to be himself and not an echo of Phil.

As Lin's problems preyed on his mind he curled up in himself, so his work suffered and his school reports were so bad that his father grew angry. Life itself seemed no longer worth having. Then Lin saw a Samaritan poster that said 'Everybody Needs Someone', and he rang the number it gave.

Now, at last, Lin was no longer a twin. The Samaritan, Mike, treated him like the real, individual person he was. Problems like Lin's don't get solved overnight but Lin no longer worries so much and he enjoys life more.

Sue

Sue's parents had split and her father had gone to live abroad with his new wife. They had a small family of their own and though her Dad wrote to her at Christmas and for her birthday, Sue still felt a terrible need of him.

When her mother married again, Sue was glad at first because she liked Len, but as she reached her mid-teens he grew stricter with her. If Sue was home later than ten from a sixth form disco her stepfather shouted and raved. It all came to a head the night of the end-of-term party. Sue explained at home that all her friends were going, and some of the teachers, and she begged to be allowed to stay out until midnight. After all, she was seventeen and she wouldn't cycle home alone; several of her pals lived in the same street.

No use. Len refused to allow her to be home later than ten . . . and the party didn't start until eight! It was a great party. Sue enjoyed it to the very end . . . midnight. She waved her friends goodbye at her gate, then found she was locked out. True, she had a door-key but the bolts were across and nobody came when she threw pebbles at the windows.

Too proud to ask neighbours for shelter, Sue slept in the cycle shed and next day she walked into the Samaritan Centre, saying she wanted to leave home . . . run away . . . escape.

Mary talked it through with Sue, calmed her temper, tried to help her see things in perspective. She began to understand the special responsibility her step-father felt for her. By the time Sue left school for university things were better all round. Mary became a real friend, and Sue felt her way to a better relationship with the adults in her life. Now university seems not so much an escape route as a new experience, but she knows she'll be glad to come home for the vacs. . . .

Conclusion

Everyone feels desperate at times. Most of us have someone to turn to — a relation, a friend, a teacher. For those who feel truly alone, the Samaritans are always available, always ready to listen.

11
Fair trading

Aim

To look at trading standards and the way we expect fair treatment.

Props

A garment which is obviously too small for the owner. A large balloon and metric tape measure. A pair of high-heeled shoes with one heel off.

Collage

Use posters borrowed from the Office of Fair Trading to decorate a wall or board.

Facts

● *Find out from books* Obtain, by post or call, leaflets from your Office of Fair Trading . . . they cover many subjects. (You'll find the address in your telephone directory, under the name of your local council.)

● *Find out from people* Ask your friends and family if they have felt they've had a 'bad deal' and what steps they've taken to find justice. If you can visit the nearest Office of Fair Trading easily, talk with someone there about the complaints they receive and what advice they give.

Presentation

You may have collected sufficient information from disappointed customers and from the staff at the Office of Fair Trading, to prepare a sequence on your own lines.

If time is short or material is hard to gather, consider the following situations and decide if you want to use them straight, think up your own, or present some kind of role-play with the ideas you have.

A pupil may arrive with a garment which is obviously too small. He says it shrank in the wash, although the washing instructions were carefully followed. Has he cause to complain? If so, what should he do first? He should take the garment back to the shop, with the receipt if he still has it. . . .

A girl brings a pair of high-heeled shoes which are a disaster — one heel is off! She says the manager of the shop where they were bought doesn't wish to know . . . he blames her for 'improper use!' What can you use shoes for, other than walking? What should this pupil do now? How do you discover the maker's name, to complain to the firm? In the Directory of Trade Marks. . . .

Another pupil says her mother lost a day's work waiting at home for a man who promised to come to repair her washing machine. Remember that Fair Trading covers services as well as goods!

A student brings a balloon he bought for the school disco . . . the packet says it will inflate to 100 cm. . . . Blows it up and measures . . . it falls short. Is the balloon faulty or does he have too little puff?

These are the kind of complaints the Office of Fair Trading deals with all the time. They test petrol pumps to make sure that when the meter reads a gallon, you get a gallon. They weigh coal to check you get the right weight. They keep an eye on dairies to make sure there's really a pinta in your bottle.

Some people are always complaining . . . but it's just as well that there is an organisation to protect us, because Fair Trading is important.

Is fair trading one-sided? If we skip our homework are we trading fair? If we forget a dental appointment, have we taken a place someone else needed?

We all depend on each other for Fair Trading. . . . Be your own Watchdog — Trade Fair!

Conclusion

We all get steamed up when we think people are not fair to us. How fair are we in our dealings with others?

12
Fingerprints

This can be topical if there are current press reports of a crime solved by fingerprints.

Aim

To emphasise the way we are all different and show how everything we touch in the course of a day bears our mark.

Props

Take your own thumbprints and those of some of your friends, and try to enlarge them so that their differences will be visible when on display. If this is too difficult ask your neighbourhood community affairs policeman to give or lend you a few posters showing fingerprints.

Facts

● *Find out from books* Most libraries have many books, fact and fiction, about fingerprinting used to identify a criminal. Find out when this method of detection was first used and all you can of its history.

● *Find out from people* Ask at your local police station if you may question the officer about the use of fingerprinting. You may be able to get permission to invite him to school to talk briefly about the use of fingerprints in his job. The Community Affairs Department will almost certainly send someone to address your assembly.

Presentation

If you have been fortunate enough to gain the help of a police officer, he or she will demonstrate fingerprinting techniques and talk about their use in crime detection.

Or you may decide to relate what your own research has revealed. Remember that there are ways to avoid identification . . . a criminal may wear gloves to conceal his prints.

This would be more interesting if you could devise a playlet or even a mime to illustrate your points. You could envisage a scene in a school office, a house, or a teenager's own room, which had been ransacked by an intruder. At least three characters are needed in the room . . . one to dial 999 . . . another to attempt to clear up the mess . . . the third person must emphasise that everything should be left as it is until the police arrive.

Enter the PC or DC, with notebook . . . when the notes are completed he or she will press the occupant's thumb and fingers onto an inked pad and transfer them to a tape or other material for safe keeping.

Discuss with the police person the reason for recording the owner's prints and learn that this is to eliminate legal prints. Police remind us that we all leave our mark on almost everything we touch.

Then table-top, books, etc. are covered with fine powder and the marks revealed are 'lifted' onto tape, which the police explain will be compared with known 'villains' marks.

When the police have gone, the characters remaining discuss fingerprints. Emphasise how these are all different . . . just as we see things differently, so the mark we leave varies. Only the person who has worn gloves has covered his tracks, leaving no marks.

Conclusion

Many people have lookalikes, but in minute details we are all different. Fingerprints reveal the uniqueness of human beings. They also remind us that we can't go through life without leaving our own special impression on things, people and events. We leave our mark every day . . . not just on school exercise books, but on the classes we attend, the games we share, the people we meet. Only those who withdraw from society, refusing to join in, are wearing gloves, and they become sadly anonymous.

13
Flight bag

This is topical when there is news of a mass refugee situation, or on 1-3 September, the anniversary of the days in 1939 when many school children found themselves evacuees.

Aim

To decide what is really important in our lives, and what material things, if any, we'd want to keep in an emergency.

Music

'Favourite things', from *The Sound of Music,* and many other songs feature the items which are precious to people.

Poetry

Rupert Brooke's poem 'The Great Lover', which you will find in many anthologies of twentieth century poetry, would be appropriate. You might enjoy writing your own poem on this theme!

Props

Take one flight bag and fill it with the things you feel are essential in a refugee situation. You may find some of the ideas which follow are useful: they were contributed by three teachers and seven pupils at a secondary school.

Facts

There are no facts for you to find for this assembly — only the ideas you have yourself or can gather from friends. Have fun with this one . . . and think deeply too.

Presentation

The *Desert Island Discs* programme confronts a celebrity with a tantalising choice: he or she must select eight records, one book and one luxury to last an indefinite time on a desert island.

Imagine that your situation is even more desperate: you have to leave home, at minimal notice, with just enough of your precious possessions to fill a flight bag.

Many refugees, worldwide, forced into sudden flight, face this kind of dilemma. Some of the staff of this school may even have had to pack their bags for evacuation to safer areas at the start of World War Two.

To ease your choice, it is assumed that you will be fed and cared for, so you need no food, clothes or sponge bag . . . just take whatever is most precious in your life. Maybe you will concentrate on the past, taking memory-joggers, or perhaps the future concerns you more. Some students, faced with this situation, have rejected the flight bag, saying they were secure in their own personalities, needing no props at all to start a new life. Let's consider the contents of this bag:

FLIGHT BAG

A map: not knowing where in the world one would arrive, it could be useful to have a map, showing rivers and mountains, towns and villages. A very practical choice.
A white mouse: pets are very important in many lives, but if we take this, the 'refugee' is responsible for another life.
Photographs: maybe these evoke more memories than anything. Will they be pictures of dead loved ones, of family left behind, or of places like former homes and schools, or beauty: 'Britain in Springtime'?
A book: something to read on a long journey, of the kind you never tire of and re-read over and again? Holy books are infinitely precious to people with faith, so the Bible or the Koran or the Torah or whatever would be essential for these travellers. Some would say this is the only essential.
Pastimes: playing cards, Scrabble, Mah Jong, chess, games to reduce boredom and also to make contact with other people. Even strangers can often join in a game, regardless of language barriers.
A football: you'd need to deflate it, or it would fill the bag, of course, but it has great potential for fitness and fun.
Seeds: a very small packet, but promising a crop of your favourite food, or of flowers to remind you of home . . . always provided the climate you find resembles the one you left.
Knife: a weapon could work two ways . . . are you taking it for self-defence or for attack? Is there any possibility of a stable life when people carry arms? But perhaps the knife is to prepare food, in which case it could be almost essential.
Musical instrument: this would have to be small . . . a Jew's harp or a mouth-organ, or even a recorder. Music, like games, can build bridges, and be a source of comfort in an alien place.
Birth certificate: this item links the past and the future. It establishes identity, proves

nationality and birthplace. It could determine your reception by the people among whom you settle.

Degree certificates, school reports: for those with an eye to the future, these may be extremely useful, proving eligibility for work. Just make sure only the best report is packed!

Diary: not so necessary if date lines are crossed — you could get very confused about which day was which! Necessary if you intend to keep a record of your new life. You might even write a book about your experiences with the help of your diary. . . .

Paper and ball-point: to write home? Your home may be forever unreachable or destroyed. But writing down your feelings, your ideas can be very constructive and helpful.

Very little: your bag may be empty or nearly so. Perhaps you are so uncluttered by material things that you are willing to start a new life on the strength of your own personality. Your memories may be in your mind, your future depends on your fortitude.

Conclusion

The contents of our flight bags would be as different as we all are from each other. We have gained a small insight into the poverty in material things of many people in our world. We have also realised how very little of all the material comforts we enjoy are really essential to us. Think about this next time you feel hard-done-by!

14

Harvest

It is important to remember that this will be topical not only in autumn, the season usually associated with harvest in Britain. People with roots in other countries may celebrate harvest at different times.

Aim

To celebrate the food of the world.

Props

Bring a mini harvest display, using locally grown food with special emphasis on the harvest of ethnic groups in the school. A string of ground-nuts would be attractive, so would a pineapple, melon or coconut. Make a background of posters from Christian Aid or any other development agency.

Reading

Two hymns, found in most hymn books, would make appropriate readings: J. Arlott's 'God, whose farm is all creation', and F. Pratt Green's 'For the fruits of his creation, thanks be to God'. If you have a non-religious theme, your librarian will help you find an appropriate poem or prose reading.

Facts

● *Find out from books* Write to Christian Aid, Secondary Educational Advisor, P.O. Box No 1, London SW9 8BH for their information packs. They have a leaflet for use in school assemblies called Feeding the Human Family, and can provide a great deal of information.

● *Find out from people* Ask anyone who has lived abroad about harvest in other countries. Remember this will range from grapes in Germany and tea in Sri Lanka, to sugar cane in Jamaica.

Presentation

1. You may wish to make this a traditional, homespun celebration with one or two familiar harvest hymns. This could be a thanksgiving service, recognising that however hard people work to produce the food they need, harvests come from seed, sunshine, rain, soil, which are the gifts of God.

2. On a more secular note you could invite people who, if asked in good time, would talk about a harvest less well-known to most hearers. It would be interesting to learn how many things we take for granted are harvested . . . coffee, rice, peanuts. . . .

3. You may wish to emphasise how non-British harvests are celebrated; for

example, in South India the Hindus have a three-day festival at the season of rice harvest, in January or February. In the Punjab, in April or May, they rejoice at the winter harvest, a special dance is performed when village people dramatise their work.

4. Having taken a fresh look, and expressed our gratitude for the many foods we enjoy from all round the world, it would be appropriate to consider the whole picture and realise that not every nation is well fed.

In 1974, Henry Kissenger, who was American Secretary of State at the time, said that by 1984 no child would go to bed hungry. We know now that not only do children go to bed hungry, they die of starvation. In 1983 an article in *The Guardian* newspaper said that one person in four of the world's population suffered from chronic malnutrition. (You could count round your assembly and ask every fourth person to stand up or, if already standing raise a hand.)

If these people lived in the hungry parts of the world, they would not just be longing for a bar of chocolate or a packet of crisps, they would be needing food — and food that would fill their stomachs and give them energy to live through another day.

Yet there really is enough food in the world. It is not God's fault that people die of hunger. It is our fault . . . the sin of the whole human race . . . that we have not yet found enough love and made the effort to share the good things some of us enjoy. This is why people in the development agencies collect money and goods, send helpers abroad, supply seed and machinery, to enable families who live in poor parts of the world to help themselves. Land conservation, water management and the gift of seed can often be triggers that set a community on the way to a real harvest.

Conclusion

People of many races and beliefs use harvest time as an opportunity to give thanks for the food they eat. Many also use it as a reminder that there are needy people in the world. So harvest is often a time of giving to charity.

There have always been hungry nations in the world. In our generation we are more aware of them . . . nobody can fail to notice the pictures of starving children. Ignorance can no longer be an excuse for doing nothing. It would be wonderful if ours could be the first generation in the history of the world when nobody died for lack of food. Think of the quarter of us, in this assembly, who could be dying of malnutrition . . . imagine a time when no one lived under this threat. It's great to give thanks for our food. It would be even better if we made up our minds to work to change the way the world is organised, so that all may share in the earth's fruitfulness.

15

Here is the news . . .

Aim

To evaluate the news bulletins we hear on the radio or watch on TV.

Props

A newsreader's table, with chair and clipboard for notes. You could try taping the music or sound which precedes an actual broadcast to start the assembly, or just announce 'Here is the News . . .'

Facts

● *Find out from books* Read Jan Leeming's book, *Working in Television* (Batsford Press, 1980), or *Really Bad News,* by members of Glasgow University Media Group (Writers and Readers Publishing Co, 1982), or Julian Fox, *The Power of the Media* (Wayland, 1981). Your librarian may point you to other books about the gathering and presentation of news.

● *Find out from people* Contact the nearest radio or TV station which has an education department. Explain your interest, you may find they will offer 'inside information'. Ask people of different ages what they think of radio and news coverage, if they believe all they hear and see, and if it influences their lives.

Readings

If you are using an incident from one of the sacred scriptures in your presentation, this would be an appropriate place to read a small passage of the original account of the incident, eg:
1. The event in the Buddha's life which led to his Middle Way of Deliverance.
2. Mohammed's escape from Mecca to Medina.
3. The discovery of Christ's empty tomb on Easter morning.

Presentation
1. This assembly may be featured in a straightforward way with an explanation of the manner in which media news is gathered. You will have learned in your research that observers all round the world are sending news items to the centres of communications all the time.

   In the radio or TV centre the editors sift the news and decide upon its order of importance. Often special reporters are flown to the scene of a disaster or hi-jack so that firsthand accounts may be given. This results in very close identification with something that may be happening on the other side of the world.

   You may feel that news coverage is angled towards the sentimental or the tragic, with not enough news about the good, or even funny things that happen.

c

On the other hand, you may think that exposing people in their livings rooms to the plight of less fortunate groups makes us all aware of world problems and more willing to help. The huge efforts to aid the victims of famine in Africa began with a news item on television.

"HERE IS THE GNUS"

2. Should you decide to go for a more lively approach, you could present your own 'news bulletin'. This may be a local affair, describing the events in your school. Your headlines might read like this:

    A record number of pupils sat A level general studies exams this year.

    The B team lost to Wigglesworth High, with the score 16-15 at the whistle after extra time.

    A new *Encyclopedia Britannica* has been bought for the school library with the proceeds of the sale of lolly-sticks.

    The headmaster's wife has had twins and the science lab's rabbit had sextuplets. The head expressed pleasure that the new arrivals came to the appropriate parents. . . .

    We now go over to interview the deputy caretaker who collected the lolly-sticks from the tuck-shop rubbish bins. . . .

3. It may be more suitable for you to give your own version of the day's national and international news, with its challenge of presenting known facts in your order of importance.

4. Another idea would be to take the reading you selected from a holy book and re-write it like a modern news bulletin. A reporter could give an eye-witness account of the events as the Buddha sat under the tree, or Mohammed escaped from Mecca, or the scene in the garden when the empty tomb is discovered. . . . There are many alternatives in most religious narratives. For Christian assemblies in a school with a lively domestic science department, a better illustration from the life of Jesus might be his appearance by the lakeside, when

he prepared breakfast for his friends. Peter could be interviewed and a TV cook could comment on the barbequed fish!

However you present your news, make it immediate and impressive.

Conclusion

There is rarely a day in the year when we do not receive media news. We can ignore it by not switching on, and we can switch off, but the news goes on, every day. It is for us, the listeners and viewers to make our own decisions and act upon or ignore, the events that happen in our world.

16
The Highway Code

This would be topical if used with a group who are planning to learn to drive or to take their test. It could also be useful if new traffic laws are passed by parliament or if there is a special local concern about road use. Otherwise, it can be presented at any time of year.

Aim

To discover that nobody can be counted-out where road safety is concerned.

Props

A copy of the Highway Code. A crash helmet. Enlarged copies of road signs from the *Highway Code.* You may choose the Road Works triangle, the No Motor Cycle circle and the Falling Rocks triangle, but the choice is yours. . . .

Facts

● *Find out from books* Read the *Highway Code* thoroughly. A book on the history of motoring will reveal some humorous and interesting facts.

● *Find out from people* If you can persuade your local Traffic Policeman to talk with you, many facts about local problems will emerge. Ask particularly about accident figures involving scooters and motorcycles and mishaps to people on foot.

Presentation

Driving tests, like school exams, are part of everyday life for many of us. It pays to prepare and to take time to get things right. A great deal may depend on the results.

If you have interviewed the traffic policeman you will be well-armed with facts and figures and may prefer to tackle this topic your own way. If time or ideas are short, the following script should be a guide to presenting an assembly on the Highway Code.

SCENE . . . A school common room where a group of pupils are discussing a forthcoming driving test.

Jon has been having driving lessons and has asked his friends to test him on the Highway Code.
Cilla is a cyclist.
Becky is a pedestrian.
Steve joins them later, wearing his crash helmet.

Jon	Come on girls, ask me a few more questions, then I'll buy you a Coke.
Cilla	OK. What's your stopping distance on a dry road at 60 mph?
Jon	That's easy. 175 feet.
Cilla	Wrong! It's 240 feet. I guess it's always more than you think.

| Becky | My life could depend on your knowing how soon you can stop. When I walk to school I often wonder if motorists really could stop quickly if the heel came off my shoe as I crossed the road. |

Becky My life could depend on your knowing how soon you can stop. When I walk to school I often wonder if motorists really could stop quickly if the heel came off my shoe as I crossed the road.

Cilla What is this sign telling you? (Holds up the large Road Works triangle).

Jon It's a man struggling to open an umbrella. (All laugh.) No, it means road works ahead, and it's a warning sign. Now try me on an order sign, that must be obeyed.

Becky (Holds up the No Motor vehicles sign as Steve enters.)

Steve (removing his helmet . . .) No flying motor bikes allowed. I've left mine outside!

Jon It's no motor vehicles of any sort, no messing. This is not a maybe, it's an order.

Steve I hate all these orders. Do you know there's even a section of the Highway Code for pillion passengers and musts and must-nots for cyclists and scooter riders.

Cilla But the rules are for everyone's good, we all have to study the Highway Code for our own sakes, and other people on the Road.

Becky I don't. I haven't even got a bike. It's bad enough having to learn so much at school, at least I don't have to read about how to cross the road.

Steve Oh yes you do, Becky! In fact, the very first part of the Highway Code is for you. Show her, Cilla . . . the road user on foot. Five and a half pages, just for you.

Jon No, not just for Becky . . . for all of us. We are all pedestrians at some time. Like most of the Code, these rules are for everyone. People just don't realise that they could be a danger to another person, even if they are on foot.

Becky One more question, then we'll go for those Cokes. (Holds up the Falling Rocks sign.)

Steve I know that one . . . the natives are not friendly!

Jon This native will get you if you don't let me concentrate. Beware falling rocks. Though I guess I'm in more danger from careless pedestrians than from a landslide.

Becky Makes you think, doesn't it? Can I borrow your Highway Code, Jon, I'd like to read the bit for Road Users on Foot.

Jon Sure thing . . . but not until after Friday, when I hope to get rid of the L Plates. Four cokes, OK?

Cilla It does make you think. Most things that people do together involve us all in some kind of responsibility. Was it John Donne who said 'No man is an island?'

Steve There's a bit in the Code about approaching islands . . . or is it roundabouts . . .?

Becky My Mum says life is all swings and roundabouts, I suppose she mean's were all in it together!

Conclusion

Most of us ignore the Highway Code much of the time. When we are to take a driving test we study it carefully, knowing there will be questions on it however well or badly we do on the day. Yet when we are walking we seem to forget that the first section of the Code is for us pedestrians. In other words, on the street as well as in many areas of life, we need to be more responsible than we like to think!

17
Honesty

Aim

To show that we all need to be honest, all the time.

Props

For the role-play: chairs, kettle, coffee, cups or mugs, ball-point.

Facts

● *Find out from books* Statistics on theft (*Annual Abstract of Statistics*, Central Statistical Office, available from most reference libraries).

● *Find out from people* Ask policemen, shopkeepers about theft. Your school librarian will tell you how many books disappear from the library each year.

Readings

Use something about honesty from as many scriptures as you can find. See books marked with an asterisk in the General Booklist, p. 117.

> *The Hindu Yama* says 'Do not lie . . . do not steal'.
> *The Raja Yoga* says 'Abstain from harming others, from falsehood and theft'.
> *Sikh* commandments include speaking the truth.
> *The Islamic Sharia* rejects dishonesty.
> *The Ten Commandments* reflect Jewish and Christian thinking on honesty.
> *The New Testament* comment includes Matthew 22:37-40: Love your neighbour as
>   yourself.

Music

Many popular songs reflect the need for honesty in speech and action.

Information

Everything we buy in the shops could be ten per cent cheaper! So a £5 LP could cost you £4.50! Then why do we all pay so much more than we need? How can we get prices down? The answer is simple — we pay too much because some people take goods without paying. In other words, they steal. We would have less to pay if we stopped the shop-lifting, fiddling, and other ways of stealing that are robbing us all, every day.

There are many ways of stealing — filling in forms for social benefit, or a claim for reduced income-tax are opportunities to be dishonest. If everyone made completely honest claims, we'd almost all be better off! But that would be too good to be true, wouldn't it? People go on fiddling their forms, and stealing from shops.

You have probably found some startling facts in your research, maybe about your own school or neighbourhood, that you wish to quote.

SHOP LIFTING IS DISHONEST

Role-play

(Bring this right up-to-date by using examples that are local and/or topical.)

Group of pupils are having coffee and discussing homework.

Greg   I've got this essay to write about (elections, famine, disaster).

Sue   I saw a TV programme about that last night . . . there was a lot of information.

Greg   You're a big help! I was playing badminton last night . . . I didn't even watch the news.

Stuart   There's a super book on your topic in the school library. I saw it last week when I was looking up (a linked subject). . . . I think there's a resource pack and a tape as well as reading material. If you ask the librarian, I'm sure you'll get help.

Sue   That's not on. I heard the librarian wailing that somebody had taken that pack without signing it out. I guess nobody will ever see that in school again. It will be like the track suit I left in the changing room, gone, but not forgotten.

Greg   (angrily) That's rotten! It's stealing! How could anyone be so mean! If there's one thing that makes me mad, it's people who take things that don't belong to them.

Stuart   One of our neighbours bought that info-pack — if someone will lend me a pencil, I'll make a note to ask if I can borrow it for the night.

Greg   You're a pal, Stu! Have my ball-point.

Stuart   Your ball-point! This says 'Property of Exchester Post Office'! It's printed down the side. You stole this, Greg. No wonder I can never find a pen when I'm in there!

Greg   Come off it . . . taking biros from Post Office counters isn't stealing. I must have just put it in my pocket without thinking.

Sue   I read somewhere that everything would cost a lot less if everyone were honest. Every time someone takes something that's not theirs, someone else suffers.

Greg   OK. I'm convinced. I'll return the ball-point on my way home. And I promise not to keep that info-pack a minute longer than I need!

Conclusion

All the major faiths teach honesty as a basic commandment, but how convinced are we that this applies to us? Today's a good time to decide to deal honestly with everyone, in all situations.

18
Hooked!

This will be topical on National Non-Smoking Day or when addiction is news for one reason or another.

Aim

To look at addiction — excessive drinking, smoking and drug abuse — and its effect not only on the addicts, but on their families and even on strangers.

Props

Posters and leaflets may be obtained from The Health Education Council, 78 New Oxford Street, London WC1 1AH, or from your local Health Education Officer or your Area Health Authority. (Get the address from the public library.) The more you tell them about your project, the more useful will be the material you receive.

Facts

● *Find out from books* *Addiction in the News* by Vanora Leigh (Wayland, 1983) and *So You Want to Try Drugs?* by Fiona Foster and Alexander McCall Smith (MacDonald, 1981).

Read back copies of local and national papers at your nearest library — there may even be a file at your school. Collect all the evidence you can find on traffic and other offences caused by addiction, or just from 'one drink too many'.

● *Find out from people* Ask a community policeman or a social worker if they can give you any information on the sadness caused by drug and alcohol abuse.

Presentation

Everybody wants to get the most out of life . . . especially young people. Suddenly, when we are round about eleven or twelve, we become aware of all the opportunities life offers, thrills, new experiences, adult interests, and we can hardly wait to get involved in things we've seen grown-ups doing for years.

Are all adults worth imitating? Most of us have seen people, even in their early twenties, with bad teeth and dreadful coughs, lighting up yet another cigarette. Why? Because they're hooked on smoking.

Some of us know people who own cars and motor bikes the law won't let them drive. Why? Because their abuse of alcohol led to an accident and they were banned from driving.

We may even know people whose bodies are unfit and minds confused, not because they were born with an incurable disease, but because they are also hooked — on drugs.

Of course, we may be lucky. We may live in a family, a neighbourhood, where nobody suffers from any of these self-induced ills, but we can't escape facts.

Consider these cuttings from newspapers. . . . (*This will have most impact if several voices read in turn.*)

These three young people lived in the same small town. They all came from very ordinary, happy homes, but they were hooked! Their names have been changed, of course. . . .

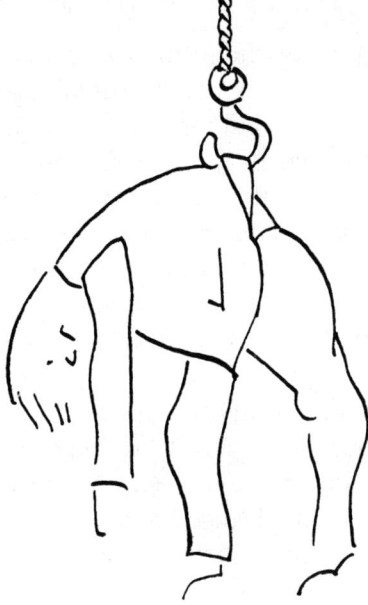

HOOKED

Stuart   He had just left school. He was one of the unlucky ones, no job and not much money. He was lucky in a way, because he had a good-looking girlfriend, and he'd learned to drive when he was seventeen. Not that he and Mel went out in a car very often. Neither of their Dads was keen on lending their car, and anyway the petrol was too dear. One winter night, Stuart and Mel were fed up — bored. Then he had an idea. His elder brother had left his car at home, because he'd gone to a party and knew that if he drank there he might not be able to drive home.

Mel was a bit doubtful about Stu borrowing the car without permission, but, as he said, there was nobody at home to ask. . . . So they drove to a pub and had a few drinks, then, on the way back, they stopped for a few more. When their money was all gone, they made for Mel's home but they didn't arrive. Instead, a policeman came, to say that Mel and Stu were in hospital . . . the car had gone down over a bank; they were lucky to be alive. Mel was badly injured, she's still in constant pain, and Stu was in real trouble with the law. He'll never forgive himself for what he did to Mel that night . . . she was a super girl and now she won't even look at him. Finding a job will be even harder for him and his parents seem to have aged by years. . . .

Janis   All Janis really wanted was to have a husband who loved her, a home of her own, and a baby, or two, or three. And a cigarette, or ten, or twenty. Janis was married at eighteen, and when she was nineteen she held her first baby in her arms, but only once. Janis' baby only lived for hours. He was premature, and tiny, and too ill for the doctors to save his life. Everyone was very kind to Janis, but she knew she'd killed her baby, because she hadn't loved him enough to give up smoking; she was hooked. Maybe her story will have a happy ending. Janis has decided that she will never smoke another cigarette — in her eyes they are killers.

Tony   He was one of those people who seem to have everything. Parents who had plenty of money and adored him. An apparently unfailing ability to pass exams, he was usually not just top of his class but top of his year. But Tony was no swot, he was captain of games, and had medals and prizes for out-of-school activities. Tony knew where he was going . . . to medical school, then to be a surgeon, and everyone said he'd make it. The trouble was that no one knew that in the sixth form Tony discovered drugs. Not the kind to help people, the sort he'd learn to prescribe in hospital. Tony's drugs made him feel great — at first. Then he began to feel awful, really ill. His work went downhill and his A level results were not good enough to get him a place anywhere.

So Tony disappeared. Just opted out of the life he'd known. His parents tried to trace him, his friends were questioned, but Tony had gone. Years later, they found him, but it was too late. He'd died at twenty-one, of drug abuse. Not an overdose — Tony didn't intend to kill himself. He died because the very substance that made him feel so good had done no good at all. He'd been unable to get off the hook. . . .

These may sound extreme examples — they are only too common, reflected in different but similar circumstances round the world. The world which is so exciting for most young people is ruined for some by their own inability to say NO.

Conclusion

We live in a wonderful but dangerous world. We can't plead ignorance of either its opportunities or its dangers. Very few people get through life without being tempted in one way or another. At least we are living in an age when the temptations that would hook us are well known, when we can see the consequences of our actions. In the end, it's up to us . . . a fish doesn't have to swallow the tempting bait, and we can ignore the cigarettes, the drink, the drugs which might lead us into danger. In the end, it's all up to us. . . .

19

It's not what you do, it's the way that you do it

End-of-term, when some pupils will be leaving school, would make this topical. A strike, national or local, could also focus attention on work.

Aim

To appreciate that work of many kinds can be useful to society as well as a way of earning money. Out-of-work time need not be wasted time.

Props

Collect all the interesting job advertisements you can find. Distribute them among pupils at the assembly who are willing to call out the name of their 'work' at a given point.

Music

Choose a suitable song from the many that refer to work.

Reading

There are many poems about work in anthologies. Ask your librarian to help you find one that expresses what you want to say.

Facts

● *Find out from books* Ask your careers teacher or the officer at your local careers centre for books or pamphlets about work. You may find many jobs you'd never heard about, some with very odd titles.

● *Find out from people* Ask a grandparent, or someone else you know who has worked at the same job for many years, how they feel about work. Talk with a teenager who is unemployed and discover how he or she spends the day.

Presentation

This assembly could feature a dialogue, with two people discussing the problems of leaving school and finding a job. It could also be presented 'straight' with people from the group contributing their 'work' at the given time.

Probably the most hated question that adults ask young people is — 'What will you be when you leave school?'. A first-year pupil at a secondary school replied instantly . . . 'a film star'. Well, Gina Lollobrigida made it. True, this pupil is fat and plain, but so was Gina Lollobrigida once.

Many of us feel that this is not a matter we can decide. Jobs are scarce, so we take what we can and make the most of it. Happily careers teachers and staff at job centres help a lot. There are jobs that deal with life from the cradle to the grave, from midwives and doctors to undertakers and grave-diggers. Listen to some of the things people do for a living. . . .

(The list is read from the pupils' slips of paper. . . .)

Copper-bottomer

Back washer

Road doggy

Gut twister

Vamp creaser

Quilt banger

Potato peeler

Under-overlooker

Sausage linker

Puff-putter-in

There must have been some jobs there you'd never heard about. Yet it seems they are all needed. There'd be no bangers and mash without the sausage linker and the potato peeler!

So does God come into all this at all? Are all jobs blessed by him? Is all work worthwhile? How about the cat burglar, the drug pusher, the cigarette manufacturer?

We should not imagine that some jobs are more important than others, simply because they earn more money. Is a doctor more important than an electrician? We need both . . . we all depend on the work of many other people, every day.

A woman in a bus was nagging her son for not doing his homework. 'If you don't get good CSE's you'll end up a dustman.' The boy looked from the bus window at the bags of rubbish in the street. Dustmen were on strike and the people in the houses had to smell rotting vegetables and risk disease. We need the service jobs, like rubbish collecting, nursing, banking, teaching. We also need the productive jobs like making scooters, TV's and computers.

The point is that most jobs need doing — and doing well. A pay-packet is a symbol of hard work, done for money, but it also marks a contribution to life, to helping others to live, in various ways.

What if there's no work, if you have to go on the dole? Paid employment is not the only kind of work. Many societies and groups need willing people who have something that's very precious — time to spare. Sometimes the jobs people do for free are the most needed, and most rewarding.

Conclusion

Most work helps not only the worker, but other people too. We need to look at employment in a broad way and determine that whatever we do with our time, we will do a good job.

20
Life like a silent film

Aim

To understand the barriers of foreign languages or of deafness: to try to 'say it without words'.

Reading

Choose any suitable passage or poem, but read it soundlessly . . . using lips but not voice, or ask someone to read in a language foreign to the group, e.g. in Hindu or in Russian.

Display Material

Send for one of the information posters or publicity posters available from the Royal National Institute for the Deaf (see Addresses of Organisations, on p. 121). These are listed in their publications list, together with much other material.

Facts

● *Find out from books* Send for some of the leaflets in the RNID list — *Deaf and Hearing People,* which is designed for schools, would be a good choice. Read a life of Beethoven or another well-known person who was deaf. Helen Keller, the great American, was blind and deaf, but her story is so well known it will have less impact.

● *Find out from people* If you know somebody who is deaf, perhaps you can learn from them about the problems and how they may be overcome. It would also be helpful if you could talk with somebody who is not deaf but has communication difficulties because they do not speak English and so do not understand the speech of those around them.

Presentation

The silent 'reading' of your chosen passage will have given your group a chance to imagine what it is like to be deaf, or totally uncomprehending of a language. To live in such a silent, uncommunicating world must be lonely and frustrating. Centuries ago this was appreciated by Juan Pablot Bonet, of Madrid. In 1620 he devised a series of hand signals which form the basis of the sign language which is a great help to deaf people round the world today.

You may like to have someone who will demonstrate every letter of the standard manual alphabet, which is on a card issued by the RNID. Or perhaps you could persuade two people to talk briefly in sign language . . . simple words like 'Hello, how are you? What is your name?' and so on. . . .

This may have been the idea behind another kind of non-verbal alphabet

LIFE LIKE A SILENT FILM

prepared for use between people who do not speak the same language. It was created for people who came from different cultures and faiths to the fourth World Assembly for Religion and Peace held at Nairobi in 1984. There were altogether about six hundred people from sixty different nations there, so you can imagine how difficult it was for them to talk with each other, or even greet each other. A small group was asked to think about appropriate communication that would help friendship and understanding in these circumstances, and one of its members had an inspiration: the wordless greeting they devised has since been used in many parts of the world, including India, Thailand, Japan, America and Great Britain.

With a little practise, two of your friends could soon learn the actions for this wordless greeting while you 'interpret' the signals. Actions are printed in capitals. Explanation in small type.

I OFFER YOU PEACE. Hands held about shoulder height, elbows at sides, hands facing forwards.

I OFFER YOU LOVE. Hands scooped as if scooping your heart out, and offering it, from the centre of the chest. Finally cupped hands side by side in gesture of offering, keeping it mid-chest level, not higher.

I OFFER YOU FRIENDSHIP. Hold out hands, clasped, as if shaking hands with yourself.

I SEE YOUR BEAUTY. Begin with first one or two knuckle joints to your closed eyes. Then open eyes and hands simultaneously so that you are looking with joy at the other person over your hands — palms facing you. (It is important to keep eye contact from now on.)

I HEAR YOUR NEEDS. Cup your hands behind your ears and listen.

I FEEL YOUR FEELINGS. Hug yourself, thinking you are hugging the other person.

MY WISDOM COMES FROM A HIGHER SOURCE. Raise your right hand above your head, almost fully stretched above your right ear, palm facing the other person. First two fingers straighter, others more bent. Bring your hand down, showing the path of an inspired idea, past your temple and ear to your upper chest then bring the hand forward until your arm is almost unbent. At the same time bring your left hand forward at a slightly lower level, palm facing upward, so that both hands meet in front of you, slightly above waist level, and arms fully stretched.

I SALUTE THAT SOURCE IN YOU. Make this movement continuous with the last gesture so that as your fingertips and edges of your hands meet they treasure the 'wisdom' received. Bring your hands to centre, fingertips near lips as in the Indian salute, hold eye contact with the other person as you bow your head, and believe the thought as you do the action.

LET US WORK TOGETHER. Hands clasped with fingers interlocked, palm to palm in front of you and held out to the other person.

Conclusion

To be 'deaf to the world' is a very isolating situation. It can happen to the physically deaf and to those with language problems, yet hands can convey much more than we think. . . .

21
Life-sharing

This assembly may be used at any time. It will be topical when publicity, local or national, features spare-part surgery.

Aim

To consider the life-changing opportunities of carrying a donor card.

Props

Posters and leaflets from the Department of Health and Social Security. Try to obtain these locally, otherwise write to The Director of Information, Department of Health and Social Security, Alexander Fleming House, Elephant and Castle, London SE1 6BY. Write for booklets etc. to Royal National Institute for the Blind (address at back of this book).

Music

There are many songs connected with the body ... choose one as your introduction.

Facts

● *Find out from books* Look up transplant surgery in one of the science reference books in your library. The *New Junior Encyclopedia of Science* has a clear explanation of what is involved. You can obtain a leaflet called *Transplants for a better life* from DHSS (Leaflets) Stanmore, Middx. HA7 1ZZ. There is no necessity to send postage for this material, just write a letter explaining your needs.

● *Find out from people* Approach the staff of your nearest hospital and ask if the facts can be explained to you. With your teacher's permission, it is possible that a doctor or hospital administrator would come to the assembly to explain the subject.

Some religious groups prohibit the use of a donor service. Ask a Jehovah's Witness, for example, the reasons for this prohibition.

Presentation

Tired of pictures of starving children? Fed up with appeals for the suffering? Most of us feel like that at times, but we are also aware of the many good things we have, which others can't share.

Take benefits, for example. You have only to read booklet FB2/Nov '84 to find how many assets are on offer. Some won't apply to us, just yet, like retirement pensions or unemployment benefit, but most of us use at least some of them. Health care, student grants, all kinds of opportunities are available to help us live healthy and fairly worry-free lives.

Have you ever wondered what we can do for other people? Most schools have pet charities, for which they organise sponsored events, fêtes, or even pay for the privilege of dressing up in weird clothes one day a year.

This is great, but is it enough? Maybe you feel you have little to give . . . pocket money doesn't go far, these days. . . .

One other way you can help somebody else is very special indeed. It is to carry a universal Donor Card. This means that if, unhappily, you should die, surgeons could use the parts of your body that you had specified on the card to give new life, or sight, or health, to somebody else. If you are under 18, your parent's permission would be sought.

You may be thinking that this is a very sombre sort of thought to start a day . . . look at it the other way round. You could be the one who needs a new heart, or liver, or part of an eye! Bodies are precious . . . we only have one each, and they are the most special and most generous gift of all.

This is a true story about a young school teacher, Audrey, who lives in the Midlands. After her training she'd gone to Africa for Voluntary Service Overseas, because she felt that she'd had many privileges and she wanted to share them with people in less advantaged places. When she returned to England she found a job teaching biology in a school. Then she met her husband and they settled down to a happy married life. . . .

But Audrey's is not a happy-ever-after story . . . not yet. She began to have dreadful headaches, and finally discovered that one of her eyes was in a very bad state. After much treatment and much pain, with no progress, Audrey went to a famous London eye hospital. There the doctor told her that the cornea — the window in front of her eye — was so badly scarred that it might burst at any time. Audrey had a condition which is common in under-developed countries but mercifully rare in others.

By this time Audrey had a little son, and she desperately wanted to see him properly. When the eye surgeon told her that a corneal graft was needed very soon, she tried to put off the operation. Corneas can only be replaced by cutting the transparent window from the eye of someone who has died. Unlike other spare-parts, the transfer need not be done immediately after the death of the donor, but the agreement of the donor and his or her family is needed before it is done.

Twice Audrey travelled to London, hopeful yet fearful, and twice the operation was deferred. The third time all went well, and the graft was completed. Audrey knew little about the person whose generosity and forethought had given her back her sight. She only knew that the cornea she now sees through came by train, packed in ice.

Audrey carries her own donor card everywhere now . . . as she says, she owes humanity a great debt. During the years she was teaching, twelve young people were killed, mainly in road accidents. Nothing can stop the sadness we all feel when lives with such promise end so soon. Possibly some of those students had thought about the prospect of death, some of them may have been carrying donor cards which enabled them to give strangers life and hope.

Conclusion
We live in a wonderful time; our great-grandparents would have laughed at the idea of carrying a card donating our spare parts to living people. Now, while we are fit, and hoping to live for many years, is a good time to talk this through with our families, and if they agree, to carry a card which says we belong to a great group — the Lifesharers!

22

May Day:
(The end of winter)

1 May, or the nearest Monday after that date, is often a holiday. So check whether you will be in school, and present this on the nearest possible date to 1 May.

In the northern hemisphere, May Day is also the time when winter seems really at an end. In the southern hemisphere, this could be used at the appropriate end of season time.

Aim

This assembly gives you two choices, which will probably depend on the age-group you are preparing for. Younger children will enjoy the traditional aspect — the vanquishing of winter — especially if you use a dramatic form. Older students are more likely to appreciate the Labour Day emphasis.

The aim for assembly 1 is to revive the fun as we celebrate the warmer time of the year.

The aim for assembly 2 is to consider labour, the work which contributes so much to our common good.

Assembly 1

Music

You will need tapes of noisy, discordant sounds and of sweet, spring-like notes, to play at times indicated.

Props

Ragged clothes for Winter and his friends, saucepan lids to bang, chains to rattle. Other pupils will need light clothes, bright green or in flower colours if possible. They should have posies and strings of flowers — plastic?

Presentation

May Day has been celebrated for centuries, with young people raising a huge pole and dancing round it. This was a time for festivity with young and old enjoying the longer days of spring and the new colours in the woods and fields. In many parts of Britain a maypole is still the centre of celebrations. Find out if there is one in your area and if any old customs still survive.

You may like to work on a very ancient theme, a pageant in which winter and summer fought a battle on May Day. One of the boys should be Winter, but this is not a character like Father Christmas with snowy beard, bright berries and evergreens. This Winter is dressed in dull, ragged clothes and carries leafless branches. His friends are also ragged, but they try to cheer him with music. Even this music is discordant, being made by clanking chains and banging lids.

Then, above the discordant sounds comes sweet music and Summer enters, brightly dressed, with friends in cheerful clothes. A mock battle follows which Winter loses. He is imprisoned in the garlands of flowers and Summer sits on Winter's throne.

Conclusion

The long, dark days of winter are over — summer reigns, through the light, bright days. Let us be thankful that every year we share this special time of light and beauty.

Assembly 2

Nearly a hundred years ago, in 1889, 1 May was designated Labour Day. It is celebrated in many parts of the world with parades and other festivities.

Facts

● *Find out from books* Read about work, in your library. If there is a local collection, look up the industries which have been in your area for generations, and those which are new to the district.

● *Find out from people* Ask if there is to be a Labour Day parade in your area (the police are sure to know). If your parents belong to a Trade Union ask them what Labour Day means to them.

Props

Try to collect tools from any different local industries. These will vary according to your locality but there are few places which do not have special tools or equipment for the tradespeople.

Presentation

Ideally, you should try to arrange for some of the people who use the material on display to talk about their work . . . if only one sentence. However, since most are likely to be at work when you are at school, unless they are on shifts, perhaps you could ask them to say a few words which pupils could read, or you may manage to tape what they have to say.

Another idea would be to find a few retired people who have worked in local industries. They may be very happy to come along and share their memories of working lives, and of Labour Days of the past.

It will be most impressive if you can arrange for such people to bring one of their products with them . . . you may find you have objects as different as a rug and a pocket calculator!

An alternative presentation, if you have time, would be a kind of What's My Line game, like the one on TV. . . . Ask your 'guests' or pupils taking their parts to mime their job; have a panel who, after asking a set number of searching questions, has to guess what the job is. This is a good way to focus on the work done in a community.

You will need to be very careful not to make your assembly political — this is not the time or place for political statements.

Conclusion

In common with many people round the world, today we celebrate the work of many hands and brains, the efforts of the multitude who labour so that we may live in comfort.

23
The messengers

Aim

To encourage examination of the various ways that messages reach us.

Props

Any materials you can devise for sending messages: e.g. a whistle, a white flag, electric buzzers, or even a spoon and a pan lid.

Facts

● *Find out from books* You will find many works in your school library giving information about messages. Escape stories, spy books, and chapters in encyclopedias etc. on the Marconi inventions, the Morse code, and transmission by satellite all have information about messages.

Presentation

1. *A message is useless if it is not understood.* The signal which says 'I'm in trouble and need help' is well-known to mountain rescue teams and, hopefully, to the walker who is in danger. But somebody happily walking on the fells may not recognise this message: *blow six sharp bleeps on the whistle.* If this sound is repeated every minute, it means somebody is in danger and needs help, but if the hearers don't understand the message, it is wasted.

    Send your own SOS by tapping on the pan lid, or using whatever means you have devised.

2. *Messages may not always be verbal.* Ships had no means of sound communication for centuries but they contrived to send messages by way of flags. There was a flag that said 'we have infection aboard' and another which said 'well done'. Everyone knows what this means — *wave a white flag or handkerchief . . .* 'we surrender'.

3. *Messages need to be clear.* Garbled phrases, however important their original intention, can do more harm than good. Lives have been lost and countries devastated by inaccurate messages. There is a story that a message was sent by some soldiers saying 'send reinforcements, we're going to advance'. It was passed from man to man until it reached the command post, where the officer heard, to his amazement — 'send thirty-four pence, we're going to a dance!'

4. Probably the most important factor of all is that *the messenger should be reliable.* This next passage gives a true example of a very important messenger.

    Some of the most exciting messengers in the world today belong to a group of thirty-seven well-dressed but very ordinary men. Their boss is the

Superintendant of the Corps of Queen's Messengers, who operates from the Foreign Office, in Whitehall, London. He sends the Queen's Messengers on flights round the world, visiting British Embassies and High Commissions with secret documents. The bags they carry are so vital that they occupy seats in planes, like their guardians!

This service has been in action since 1772 — well over two hundred years. Their badge is a greyhound, which hangs from the royal crest on a blue garter ribbon. There is a story that when King Charles II was in exile, he trusted the captains of two Dutch fishing boats to carry his messages across the Channel. To prove that they were reliable messengers, he gave them as identification two silver greyhounds broken off one of his dishes. Later, when Charles was restored to the throne, he suggested that the silver greyhounds should become the badge of royal messengers.

Many men apply for the job of Queen's Messenger but few are chosen. It is work that requires loyalty and tact — and a love of travel. These are very quiet messengers, but they are in no doubt of the vital importance of the messages they carry.

5. *Most faiths have messengers* who relay the truth to others. Christians know Christ as the Son of God. They treasure his words and trust his promises because they believe his messages are true. Christians are grateful for the many messengers and prophets, from Old Testament leaders to people like John the Baptist and Anna in the New Testament, but it is from Jesus that they learn what God is really like.

Jews revere prophets like Isaiah, Jeremiah, Hosea and Amos and await the coming of the Messiah.

Muslims believe that Muhammad received a special message from the angel Gabriel who told him what Allah wanted from his people. In revelations, Muhammad received the Koran, or written message, in his own tongue, and the prophet's life was dedicated to spreading the message of his God, Allah.

Conclusion

When we trust the messenger, we believe his message.

D

24
Mine rescue

This is topical on 7 September, the anniversary of the mining disaster of 1950, or at a time of national disaster. This assembly may also be used anytime, to focus on courage.

Facts

● *Find out from books* Many books deal with disasters, natural and man-made, and the courage of those involved. Write to the National Coal Board, Hobart House, Grosvenor Place, London SW1X 7AE or contact your nearest coal mine, to obtain information about pit rescues. Or approach the Central Rescue Station, NCR, 17 South Parade, Doncaster, S Yorks.

● *Find out from people* If you live in a mining area you may find someone who has experienced a pit accident and is willing to talk about it.

Presentation

If you are presenting this assembly at a time of great tragedy, you may need to arrange your facts in a hurry. They will be gathered from news broadcasts and from national or local papers. Check your facts as far as you can, and stick to them! Eye witness reports will be specially valuable.

   You may choose to focus on courage when it is not particularly topical, knowing that somewhere, every day, people are sacrificing themselves for others. If you have your own story of courage to tell, that's great . . . if not, you may glean one from the National Coal Board, a lifesaving organisation, or the news files in a library. Should time be very short, read this true account and make it into your own. You could tell the story like a newsman talking into a phone to his editor . . . this would bring it to life. Or you could make it into a conversation between two or three women waiting at the pit-head. Whatever you do, convey the drama, the patience and above all, the courage of all concerned.

The Knockshinnock disaster on Thursday, 7 September, 1950. One minute it was just a Scottish field . . . then the ground gave way, sinking under the relentless rain into the pit below. In that mine 129 men were trapped by the fallen earth. . . . Thirteen men were completely cut off; they died. The other 116 men managed to scramble clear and reach an area above the murderous sludge, where fortunately they found a phone that worked.

   The whole of Britain was stunned. Messages arrived from the King and the Prime Minister. All over the country, and perhaps the world, prayers were said for the trapped men. Groups of wives, parents and children gathered at the pit-head, waiting desperately for news. From one home alone three men had joined the afternoon shift and by the next morning hope was stretched to breaking.

Happily the phone was a vital link. From it the rescuers learned that the trapped men were cheerful but impatient to start digging themselves out. This apparently simple solution had to be stopped — gas had gathered underground and the victims could have walked into passages of death. It needed all their courage to stay where they were and wait for rescue.

Another kind of courage was shown by the watchers above. One woman, who had poured endless cups of tea for the rescuers and reporters at the colliery explained that she needed to keep busy . . . her son was 'down there'. . . .

Friday followed the Thursday of the disaster . . . then Saturday . . . and at last a new sign of hope. Some life-saving gas masks had been rushed to Knockshinnock but the trapped men would not know how to use them! David Park, a National Coal Board employee, offered to go down the mine, wearing a mask, to show the trapped miners how to use the mask so that they could get out to safety. He promised not to leave the dangerous place where the 116 were gathered until every man had reached safety.

It was an agonisingly slow business. The first man out, a nineteen year old, reached the surface at 4.00 pm on Saturday afternoon, and told the anxious crowds that the men were alright — and 'singing like linties!' The last man walked through the gas at 1.30 am on the Sunday morning.

Everyone concerned had behaved with tremendous courage. The fearful hours endured by the trapped miners can only be imagined. So can the fear of their families waiting helplessly above ground. But perhaps David Park, who was above in safety, but walked down into danger was the bravest of all. The official report of the accident, published by HMSO says:

'As conditions deteriorated and the morale of the trapped men became strained, the very gallant action of Mr David Park had a considerable steadying effect on their morale and contributed greatly to the success of the rescue.'

Conclusion

Disasters bring out courage in people who thought themselves very timid. It is one thing to face a dangerous situation bravely, when you have no choice; it is quite different to offer to go into a risky place and stay with victims until they are saved.

25
Overcoming adversity
Sir John Wilson CBE, OBE

Aim

To face the fact that although accidents happen to most of us, sometimes good can come even through personal tragedy.

Music

African or Asian music would be appropriate for this assembly.

Reading

You may like to read Milton's sonnet *On His Blindness*.

Facts

● *Find out from books* You may be able to borrow Sir John Wilson's book, *Travelling Blind*, which is sadly out of print. Write to the Royal Commonwealth Society for the Blind, Commonwealth House, Hayward's Heath, Sussex RH16 3AZ for their information material.

● *Find out from people* Someone in your group probably knows a person who has had a cataract operation on their eyes. Maybe one of your grandparents or a neighbour has been through this experience. If you can, ask them about the operation and the effect of regaining some vision, after being nearly blind.

Presentation

Accidents happen to most of us, at home, on the road, even at school. They can be unpleasant, shocking, and sometimes painful, but happily most cause only temporary difficulty.

John Wilson's accident was not like that. One rainy day in October 1931, he went to school, an ordinary happy boy, but a mishap that day left him totally blind. He was injured in the school laboratory and spent a long time in hospital where he thinks he was about the last eye patient in Britain to be treated with leeches. To return to his school was out of the question so John went first to a college for the blind, then by scholarship to Oxford University, where he gained two good degrees.

During the second world war he worked for the Royal National Institute for the Blind in London. Through this job he was invited to spend nearly a year abroad, studying the conditions of sightless people in the Middle East and Africa. He felt a great desire to help the many victims of blindness, whose problems he understood though he could not see them.

On his return from Africa, John wrote reports which made people realise that much more could be done to help blind people all over the world. He proposed the formation of the Royal Commonwealth Society for the Blind. When it was founded in 1950, with headquarters in Britain, he became its first Director. During the 1950's he travelled over half a million miles in Africa, Asia and the Caribbean, helping to establish national societies for the blind in about thirty countries.

With his wife Jean, John Wilson began the Royal Commonwealth Society for the Blind's work in three rooms, so filthy that they had to scrub them out to make them fit for use. The Society planned mobile clinics which would travel from village to village in underdeveloped countries performing cataract operations on people whose sight was nearly gone. The blind men and women are led to the clinic by friends, and after a quick and efficient operation they are taken to recover in tents, huts or any available centre. Conditions are seldom ideal, but by the time the team moves on many people will have their sight restored.

Another area of concern for the Society is preventable blindness in young children. Often their blindness is accelerated by treatment that actually makes things worse. The Society packaged its healing eye-cream attractively and made it available at very low cost, so that local healers could afford it and make use of it. The Society tries not only to aid those who are afflicted, but also to spread information and knowledge that will help avoid blindness.

John's enthusiasm includes such ventures as organising a climb up Africa's highest mountain by seven blind farmers. This feat so inspired local young people that the following year twenty-five per cent more children enrolled in schools for the blind.

The Queen knighted the founder of the Royal Commonwealth Society for the Blind: he is now Sir John Wilson, currently the senior consultant to the International Initiative Against Avoidable Disablement.

Conclusion

If you have used Milton's poem, you could comment that the poet's reaction to the tragedy of blindness was that he could only 'stand and wait'. . . .

John could have been defeated by his tragic accident at school. Instead he turned his experience into a power of good which has brought healing and hope to thousands round the world. His reaction to his own blindness has been to go out and help those whose suffering is worse than his own.

26

The penny postman
Sir Rowland Hill

This assembly would be topical on the anniversary of Hill's birthdate, 3 December 1795, or the first sale of penny stamps, May 1840. You may also like to feature Rowland Hill when there is a special stamp issue, or if you are having a stamp exhibition at school.

Aim

To underline the importance of postage stamps, which we take for granted.

Props

Large stamp albums if you can borrow these and keep them safe! Posters from the Post Office. You may be able to obtain a large copy of a Penny Black to display.

Facts

● *Find out from books* Read about Sir Rowland Hill in an encyclopedia or biography. Find out how the post was paid for in the days before postage stamps. You may find interesting stories of his work in books on stamp collecting or on the history of stamps. Write to the National Postal Museum, King Edward Street, London EC1A 1LP for information.

● *Find out from people* Try to make an appointment with the manager of the local Post Office and discover how many stamps they sell each year, how long it takes letters to reach different places in Britain and the world. Ask questions which you think will lead to interesting items for your assembly. If you cannot manage to interview a post office manager, talk to the man or woman who delivers letters to your home. You will probably find that they have had unexpected experiences in their work!

Music

There are many songs about sending letters. Choose one you like and play it.

Readings

Choose an extract from a life of Sir Rowland Hill, quoting his words. His own explanation of the need for the Penny Post may be used: 'I early saw the terrible inconvenience of being poor . . . my mother was afraid the postman might bring a letter while she had no money to pay the postage.'

Presentation

You may collect stamps yourself, or have a schoolfriend with this hobby, in which case a few words about stamps would be appropriate and interesting. Otherwise

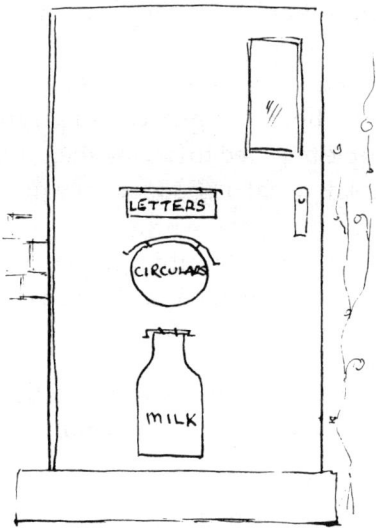

the material you have gathered from the Post Office or postman could become the subject of a 'conversation'. If you feel that postage is expensive you could work out what it costs to send a letter from, say, Cornwall to Inverness, per mile. The material from the Postal Museum should give you many ideas of your own.

If you are still short on facts, consider the life of Rowland Hill, creator of the penny stamp.

Imagine living in a time when you paid, not to send a letter, but to receive one! The cost was high but maybe you'd be willing to pay for news from someone you loved, though you might be unwilling to pay for a bill or equally unwelcome material. Not everyone had to pay. . . . Very important people like Members of Parliament could send anything through the post, just by writing their names on the parcel. Thirty hounds and a large feather bed are said to have been delivered free by this means.

While the rich managed to evade payment, the poor people waited anxiously for letters with the constant worry that they might not be able to find the cash to accept their delivery. Secret codes flourished; people arranged to mark the outside of letters in such a way that the news was conveyed without the seals being broken, so the postman had to take the unpaid packet away again.

Rowland Hill was a sickly child, who spent so much time lying down that his toys had to be hung over his bed so that he could play with them. However, he grew up to be a school teacher and later became a very active reformer. He often visited emigrant ships, crowded with people setting off for a new life in Australia. He realised that their letters home would be the only link they had with families in Britain. Gradually it dawned on Hill that a simpler way of sending news must be found.

Like many reforms, the new ideas for a postal system took time and hard work, but by 1840 the penny postal rate was ready for operation. To pre-pay the mail, people needed proof that they had handed over the cash, so Rowland Hill arranged for a competition to design a tiny sticky label . . . in other words, a stamp, the famous Penny Black.

Suddenly there was no need for a postman to knock on every door for the money before handing over a letter — houses only needed a slit cut in the door for the letter to slide through. Some people objected to having their front doors damaged in this way but in time everyone saw what a good idea the new Postal service was, and Rowland Hill was honoured round the world.

Most of us grumble about everyday things. Maybe some of them could be changed if we cared as much, and worked as hard, as Sir Rowland Hill.

Conclusion

The idea of paying to receive a letter seems very odd to us. We expect our mail to come pre-paid, but it took a man of kindness and vision to give the world the stamps we take for granted.

27
Printing
the two discoveries

This could be topical around mid-May, the time of the Triple Festival which honours the birth, enlightenment and death of the Lord Buddha, and the Buddhist New Year.

If you do not want a Buddhist emphasis, you could concentrate on Johannes Gutenberg, the European inventor of the printing press, and his bible.

Aim

To celebrate the finding of the hidden library of Buddhist texts, and the invention of printing.

Reading

Try to find a reading in English from the Diamond Sutra. One passage is printed in the *Concise Encyclopedia of Living Faiths*, see General Booklist. If you have a Buddhist temple in your area, ask if such a reading is available there. Remember to conform to the formalities of the temple: see Introduction for Pupils.

Music

Ask your school media department if a tape of Far Eastern, preferably Chinese, music is available to set the scene.

Facts

● *Find out from books* Read about the *Diamond Sutra* in an encyclopedia. Read Peter Hopkirk, *Foreign Devils on the Silk Road* (1980).

● *See for yourself* If you are in London, go to the King's Library at the British Musuem and ask to see the *Diamond Sutra*. You will view the world's first large, dated, printed book!

Presentation

We all take printing for granted, yet without it there would be few magazines and newspapers, schoolbooks or football programmes, knitting patterns or stamp catalogues. The history of printing stretches back to the distant past, and includes some remarkable and exciting events.

In the British Museum in London is the world's earliest large printed book. It was made in AD 868. We know this because the date is printed in it. This is the *Diamond Sutra*, a scroll over seventeen feet (five metres) long, with an intricately designed frontispiece or picture, showing the Buddha with a disciple. A *sutra* is a dialogue or saying attributed to the Buddha and is treasured by his worshippers.

About the time when in England, King Alfred was urging scholars to copy manuscripts by hand, six hundred years before the technique of printing was discovered in Europe, the Chinese were already printing, using wooden blocks.

Long before paper was known in the West, the *Diamond Sutra* was printed on sheets of paper mounted on a backing and rolled into a scroll. It was part of a hidden library which might have remained unknown but for a Buddhist's urge to restore part of a ruined monastery. An Emperor of China had ordered all monasteries to be demolished and their precious books destroyed. Happily, Tun-huang Monastery had fallen into Tibetan hands and its shrines escaped most of the destruction; but the careful priests walled up their library to keep it safe. There it remained, hidden, for about nine hundred years!

In about 1900 a Chinese scholar called Wang Tao-shih raised the money to restore a grotto at the monastery and, as workmen cleaned a painted wall, a crack appeared, revealing that it was made of brick, not rock. The excited scholar broke through the brickwork and found a room cut into the rock which contained thousands of manuscripts. There were silken banners, fragments of books in every Eastern language and, unlikely as it seemed, a printed scroll!

Sir Aurel Stein, a British archaeologist, was the first European to see this hidden library. In May 1907 he persuaded Wang Tao-shih to read aloud some of the words printed on the long scroll. The English traveller and the Chinese scholar agreed that this was indeed a copy of the *Diamond Sutra*. It was, in fact, the world's first real printed book. It is called *Diamond* because, as the diamond outshines other gems, this sutra is believed by many Buddhists to outshine all other written works.

Hundreds of years after the *Diamond Sutra* was printed, a German goldsmith called Johannes Gutenberg longed to find a quicker way to copy words than writing or painting them by hand. The story of the development of printing in Europe concerns Johannes Gutenberg and his friend Laurence Janzoon. Laurence was in love and he wanted to carve his girl's initials on trees. But this would make his love public and harm the trees. So Laurence carved her initials on pieces of cut green willow and wrapped them in parchment to show his beloved.

When Johannes Gutenberg saw the love token, he noted with surprise that the sap, running out of the wood, had imprinted the letters onto the parchment. Johannes hurried home to try this new idea for himself. He dipped his carved letter onto dark liquid, pressed the wood block onto a parchment and so made the first printed image in Europe. When he had perfected his first printing press, enlarging on the idea he had taken from his love-lorn friend, Johannes Gutenberg said, 'This is not a simple press, it is the mighty engine of truth. Soon it will scatter the forces of ignorance and light up the darkness on earth.'

Conclusion

Life without printing would be very different. It is one of the great assets for which most of us will always be grateful. Let us take a minute to honour the ancient Chinese scholars and the earnest German goldsmith who took time, and made the effort, to reproduce the written word by their printing processes.

28
Red Cross and Red Crescent

This will be topical on 24 June, the anniversary of the Battle of Solferino, which triggered the foundation of the Red Cross.

Red Cross day is celebrated in many countries on 8 May which is the birthday of the founder. You may find that your local Red Cross Society has a day on which it celebrates its foundation.

Aim

To consider the many roles the Red Cross and Red Crescent play in today's world.

Props

Collect cuttings from newspapers which tell of the work of the Red Cross. Scanning through the papers at your public library will reveal some that you can copy or photostat. Make them as varied as possible. Make posters showing a red cross and a red crescent.

Facts

● *Find out from books* If you are short of time, read the excellent booklet, *The Red Cross Story* by Brian Peachment, (The Religious Education Press, 1977). You will find other books about Henri Dunant and the Red Cross in your library.

Write to The Information Department, The British Red Cross Society, 9 Grosvenor Crescent, London SW1X 7EJ. Send several stamps — the literature you receive will include the story of the Red Cross and much useful information.

● *Find out from people* Locate the local Red Cross Society from your phone directory, ring to ask if somebody there will tell you what they do in your neighbourhood.

Advertise in your school bulletin, or on the notice board, for a teacher or pupil who is an active member of the Society. Find out what he or she does, and try to involve them in your assembly.

Presentation

Try to use different people to read the following paragraphs, or the selections you have chosen from newspaper accounts, which illustrate the varied nature of the work the Red Cross undertakes.

1. The young woman died at Bati. She had walked all night in bitter cold to reach the Red Cross hospital that day. She'd had no food for days. A few hours after she arrived at the camp, her baby boy was born, a healthy child in spite of all the hardships his mother had suffered. But his mother died. . . . The baby boy was

taken away by his sad father and thirteen year old sister . . . everyone in that makeshift hospital cried as they left.

2. A bridegroom — wheelchair bound — and his deaf and dumb bride were disappointed when their honeymoon plans misfired. They were delighted when the Red Cross Society heard of their plight and arranged for them to go to a Holiday Camp Centre in Norfolk. Two happy newly-weds are full of praise for the Red Cross.

3. An Iraqi man living in London received a very special Christmas greeting last year. For over twelve months he had been trying to contact his brother who is a prisoner of war in Iran. Through its international links, the Red Cross Society had managed to trace the prisoner and obtain a hand-drawn Christmas card for his family in England. This proved to them that he was still alive. Last year the International Welfare Department traced an average of one missing person every day.

4. A young man with a rare crippling disease was given a surprise twenty-first birthday treat, thanks to a Red Cross ambulance and its staff. He is a keen football fan but had never seen his team play — he's too disabled to go to a football match. Two Red Cross ambulance men called at his house to take him on a surprise trip to see his team play. They parked his wheelchair behind the goal so that he had a super view of the match and afterwards he met the players in their dressing room. They even helped him cut his birthday cake.

5. Another twenty-one year old stars in the last story . . . she, too, was at a football match. A three-month old baby at the match with its parents stopped breathing; but fortunately this young woman had been taught life-saving techniques by Red Cross members. She had learned resuscitation techniques from them for her Duke of Edinburgh Award, and gave mouth-to-mouth treatment until the baby recovered.

These five items are recorded in a recent copy of *Red Cross News*. They illustrate the many ways in which the Society helps people today.

The Red Cross was founded almost by accident. A Swiss banker, Henri Dunant, went to the village of Solferino in Italy hoping to see the French Emperor, Napoleon III. Instead, he witnessed a horrendous battle between French and Austrian forces. Henri was not the kind of man to stand back and watch people in trouble. Although he was dressed in a white suit for his meeting with the Emperor, he set about giving first aid to the wounded on both sides. The lack of organisation to care for war casualties appalled him so much that after the battlefield had been cleared he wrote a book called *In Memory of Solferino*. In it he suggested ways to remedy the situation, chief of which was to be the founding of an international society to care for casualties in war. He also proposed a treaty to give protection to the wounded and to the medics who treated them.

As so often happens, Henri's plea was part of a world-wide urge to do more to help ordinary men and women caught in a tide of war or disaster. His pleas found a willing response throughout Europe, and in October 1863 the group met which was to become the International Committee of the Red Cross.

The flag of Switzerland, where the first meeting was held, is a white cross on a red background. These colours were reversed to make the emblem which is now so familiar: a red cross on a white background. In later years, some Moslem countries found the cross symbol unacceptable, and the Society there displays a red crescent on a white ground.

The activities of this organisation are now too numerous to define. In war time the Society remains neutral, protecting victims regardless of nationality or creed. Prisoners of war are enabled to contact their families through its resources, and they often receive sustaining parcels of food and necessities. The red cross flag should guarantee immunity from attack, so that civilians and the wounded may be transported or housed in safety.

In peace time the Society is always ready to take personnel, food, blankets and the means of life to people involved in any disaster, world-wide. It trains volunteers to deal with emergencies, runs homes for the handicapped and quietly and efficiently fulfills numerous functions. It is recognised by many governments, world-wide, yet operates often on a friendly, local level. Funds are raised by many efforts, supported by volunteers.

Conclusion

Henri Dunant's vision of a society which would take quick action at times of need has been fulfilled, probably beyond his wildest dreams. The Society he founded has as its object these words:

'To inspire, encourage, facilitate and promote at all times, all forms of humanitarian activities . . . and contribute to the maintenance and promotion of peace.'

29
Rubbish!

Aim

To look at waste and consider the alternatives to the dustbin.

Props

A dustbin (clean of course), and a collection of the kind of waste you would expect to find in a family bin. Glass and plastic containers, cartons, paper and plastic wrappings, magazines, empty tins (make sure these are clean and not sharp). Other items of waste, like old toys, would be good. You could get some humour in this collection by including an item which is an in-joke at school or is topical. Small collections of glass bottles, newspapers, cans, and a jar of milk bottle tops.

Reading

Choose a passage you enjoy from *The Borrowers* by Mary Norton. There is almost certainly a copy in your school or public library.

Facts

● *Find out from books* Look up waste disposal in an encyclopedia, a book on local government, or in the careers section under Dustman. A good book, though probably a bit young for you, is *Rubbish,* by Oliver Aston (Evans Brothers, 1978). If your school has the excellent wallchart on pollution published by the World Wildlife Fund UK (11-13 Ockford, Godalming, Surrey GU7 1QU), ask if you may use it for this assembly. The front would make a good visual focal point and the back carries a great deal of useful information and addresses.

Many council waste disposal departments have good leaflets explaining their work, and items on conservation like the fact-sheets issued by the Glass Manufacturers Federation and the 'Save-a-Can' campaign organised by the Canmakers Information Department, 36 Grosvenor Gardens, London SW1W 0ED.

● *Find out from people* The collection of refuse is the responsibility of your town or rural council. Its disposal is arranged by the County Council, so you may have to 'delve' a little to find the facts you need. Start with your nearest council office, which will direct you to the appropriate person.

Think about the questions you wish to ask. They will probably include some of the following.

How much waste material is collected from this town annually?
Do you have a plant which converts the waste into useful material?
How do you dispose of the rubbish from our bins?
How many people are employed in collecting and dealing with our waste?
Is any of this refuse re-cycled?
Do we have to dispose of reusable material separately?

How can we help our dustmen?

Can you say how much of the Council's budget goes to deal with rubbish?

Presentation

You could start by tipping the rubbish from your bin onto an old sheet, and giving some of the facts you have collected. The weight of refuse a family throws away annually equals the weight of a small car! Of course, not all the kitchen waste goes into the bin. Those of us with gardens probably put this on the compost heap so that it helps to make the plants grow next year.

Could a use be found for any of the discarded material from our dustbin? *Hold up each item as you talk about it.*

Milk bottle tops, can rings: some societies, like the Guide Dogs for the Blind Association, are happy to be given quantities of these to sell to raise cash for their projects. Maybe this is something this school could do. If we represent even five hundred homes discarding two milk bottle tops daily, that would amount to a huge number of tops each term!

You may live in an area where there is a can collection, organised by the local council. The metal can often be used again, just as old cars are often crushed and the material processed to make new vehicles.

Bottles used to be reclaimed by shops and public houses; a deposit was charged to encourage people to return them. Now deposits are not usually charged, which means that many bottles are thrown away. Bottle banks are sited in many towns and some villages to encourage people to 'post' their bottles in the correct hopper — one for plain, the other for coloured glass. Most councils sell the glass collected in this way, some give the proceeds to charity; it can amount to thousands of pounds.

Paper has a much longer life than most people realise, because much waste paper can be recycled into yet more paper. Some enthusiasts, who feel that we are using too many trees to make the paper in the first place, buy only writing paper and envelopes that are made from recycled paper. Other people refuse to have their purchases put into paper bags at the supermarket checkouts when they are already securely packaged.

Many councils ask householders to make separate bundles of clean paper so that they can be sent for processing. If your dustman does not treat paper as a separate item, try to find a charity which will be glad to accept all the old newspapers and magazines you collect.

Plastic objects are really hard to get rid of — try it for yourself! Some will have surprising uses — if you cut the bottom from a squash bottle, and leave the top intact it will make a mini-greenhouse to protect a small plant from frost. But most plastic articles are useless when they are broken or empty. Perhaps this is something to consider when we are shopping — many people are refusing to buy goods which are extravagantly plastic-wrapped.

We've only looked at a few of the items in our dustbin. Think how much wider are the implications of waste, world-wide. What happens, for example, to *nuclear waste* . . . would you want it dumped near your home? The waste materials from tall chimneys may fall as *acid rain* on countries far away. Is it right that others should suffer from our sulphuric acid in this way?

Conclusion

It seems that our bin contains much less real rubbish than we expected. With a little thought and effort, we could have turned some of the contents to good use, benefiting other people. If this is true for us, it could be true for the world, but there's not much we can do, yet, to change the world. So perhaps this is the time to start with ourselves, our school, our homes, by being more careful about what we discard and by trying to care more deeply about our environment.

30
Shipwreck!

This assembly would be topical on or near 4 March (founding of the Royal National Lifeboat Institution) or when a shipwreck has made news. 6 September would also be topical for Grace Darling's exploit.

Aim

To appreciate the efforts of those who go to sea to save people in danger.

Props

Write to the Royal National Lifeboat Institution, West Quay Road, Poole, Dorset BH15 1HZ, for posters, information, etc. A poster would make a good focus for your assembly. You could also borrow a map from your geography department and mark the nearest lifeboat station to your school, or the one where the most recent rescue was mounted.

Facts

● *Find out from books* Look up the history of the RNLI in a reference book, or read about it in the material sent by the Society. Read the story of Grace Darling in a Dictionary of Biography or in a book in your school library.

Ask at your nearest Lifeboat Station, if you live on the coast, if they have a record of rescues which you could copy and read aloud. If your school is inland, ask the reference librarian at your public library to help you find a newspaper account of an exciting rescue which you could read.

● *Find out from people* If you live near the coast, or are on holiday, ask at the Lifeboat Station if somebody will tell you what it's really like to man the lifeboat. You may even know somebody who has been rescued from the sea; their first-hand story would be vivid.

Music

A recording of a rough sea, on a sound-effects tape could be used instead of music. Fingall's Cave is an obvious choice if you want a classical piece but many records and tapes evoke thoughts of the sea.

Reading

There are many good poems about the sea. If you want to use a bible reading, Acts 27 has a graphic story of St Paul's shipwreck on the island of Malta which you could read in a modern translation or tell in your own words.

Presentation

The RNLI will send you a Question and Answer Sheet which would make an excellent dialogue. It gives a great deal of information briefly and clearly.

Alternatively you may prefer to tell the story of the foundation of the Institute which is well told in the material you will receive from them.

Since many of the people featured in these assemblies are male, this may be a good occasion to talk about a young woman whose courage inspired Victorian society and focussed attention on the need to be ready to save those in danger at sea.

On the night of 6 September 1838, a young woman, Grace Darling, looked through the telescope on the tower of the lighthouse her father maintained. To her horror, she saw the bow of a wrecked ship, impaled on a jagged rock. Clinging to the wreck she could see a group of people in a perilous state. Grace knew at once that when the sea rose with the next tide they would all drown. She persuaded her reluctant father to attempt a rescue. She pulled off her long Victorian petticoat to leave her free, and took the oars of their boat herself, rowing through the heavy seas. Four survivors had died in the waves before Grace and her father reached the rock, but they managed to pull the remaining nine aboard and reached the safety of the shore with the exhausted victims.

Today there are women who help crew the inflatable lifeboats which carry out inshore rescues. Many people are saved each year from death by drowning. Here are three examples of the work of the RNLI. . . .

Two girls, stranded on a sewer outlet pipe on Seaton Beach, Hartlepool, when the tide came in, were snatched to safety.

The crew of a radio ship were also rescued, with their caged canary!

A man, unwisely swimming from a Guernsey beach too soon after a heavy meal, had a heart attack. He was dragged to safety by other swimmers, but unfortunately it happened in a bay which was completely covered by water at high tide. Some scouts who were camping nearby offered to climb the cliff steps to summon help, and an inshore rescue-boat took off the sick man from the beach just before it vanished under the tide.

Another holiday-maker who read of this rescue in the local press was delighted to take the cutting home. His town had been collecting for the Royal National Lifeboat Institution and he wanted everyone who had given to the effort to know that he had witnessed the lifeboat in action.

Sometimes, lifeboat men die in their attempts to save others from the sea. Lifeboat people get no pay . . . the Government doesn't buy their boats . . . the rescuers risk their lives because they care about people. Their boats are built and maintained by other people who never go to sea but who also care about saving lives from the waves.

Conclusion

On anniversaries or when a shipwreck reminds us, we are grateful to the men and women who are always ready to risk their lives at sea to help others. They deserve all the support we can give.

31
Special offers

Topically:

Christians may present this at Christmas to celebrate God's gift to mankind of his Son, Jesus, or at Whitsun to record the gift of the Holy Spirit.

Hindus may like to link this to Diwali, recalling the gifts and prosperity that Vishnu's consort Lakshmi brings at this time.

For *Jews* Pesach may be the occasion for recalling the gift of freedom that began when God saved the Hebrew people from Egypt.

Anytime:

It seems that believers everywhere find time to rejoice in privileges that are the special gift of God. If yours is not a faith-related assembly, remind your group that we all share many special gifts and opportunities.

Aim

To celebrate the many 'free gifts' we all enjoy and, topically, to feature the special gifts which many faiths record.

Music

There are several songs about the availability of pleasures which cost nothing, like 'The Best Things in Life are Free. . . .'

Props

Collect all the special offer coupons you can find. Many food packs have 'money-off' promises, others proffer two items for the price of one. Collect all the special offer coupons that come through the door and ask your friends to do the same. Try to make them as various as possible — for toiletries, washing powders, food and sweets, books and hobby materials.

Readings

If this is a faith-centred assembly, choose an appropriate reading from the related sacred book; see the titles marked with an asterisk in the General Booklist on page 117.

Facts

● *Find out from books* Read all you can about the faith you are featuring, if this is a religious occasion.

● *Find out from people* Ask local shop assistants how many of the special offer coupons are used by customers daily. Look through the journals in hairdressers' and doctors' waiting rooms. You'll probably find that many have special offer coupons which nobody has bothered to use.

Presentation

1. You could ask people in various parts of your assembly area to take a special offer coupon as they enter and read it out when asked. If some are rather humorous, so much the better. This could then be linked to the religious 'gift' you have chosen to feature, with a comment on why a celebration is appropriate at this time of year.

2. If this is an Anytime rather than a Topical feature, the following true story could be useful:

Have you noticed how many free gifts and special offers reach us? Some of them may have been announced today, but probably you've no time for the kind of soap sold two-for-the-price-of-one. Possibly even the sweets with the money-off flash are not your choice of chew. . . . So, for one reason or another, many of these special offer coupons will land in the bin, or be left, unclaimed, in the magazines where they appeared.

18 January is the anniversary of a very special offer indeed. On that day, in 1913, two men had a very odd bet. An actor called Tom Hearn accepted a wager that he could not stand in the middle of London and give away five pound notes in exchange for a penny.

To give himself the best possible chance of winning, Tom dressed in his oldest suit, with frayed cuffs and torn trousers. Then he went to Trafalgar Square and stood at the foot of Nelson's column, among the pigeons, with a bundle of banknotes in his hand. They were the real thing, not fakes, but when he offered them to the crowds of people in the Square, he was ignored, or treated with something like fear. In vain, Tom begged men, women and children to give him just a penny for the five pound note he offered them.

The trouble was, people were worried by this odd-looking man with his way-out offer so they hurried away, some with a smile, others with a look of pity for they thought he was mad. Believe it or not, Tom Hearn had only two customers! One's name is not recorded. The other was a Mr Scott Atkinson, who hurried to the nearest bank with the fiver he'd 'bought' for a penny. It was changed without question for five gold sovereigns. Then he knew that the note was real, because bankers are trained to spot forgeries. When Scott Atkinson told his friends the story he always said that this was the best pennyworth he'd every bought.

Think of all the people who ignored or refused Tom's offer: maybe we are rather like them. Not just in by-passing the advertising gimmicks that entice us with cheap samples and money-off coupons, but in our attitude to more lasting gifts. Very special offers like friendship and learning, and love. If we turn away from these, we lose a great deal. . . .

(For a religious occasion the significance of the gifts of God could be added here.)

Conclusion

Your investigations into special offers will probably bring their own conclusions to mind, but you will almost certainly be left with the feeling that many privileges are neglected. We even neglect some very special offers . . . friendship, learning, love . . . there are many more. Let's take advantage of them all.

32
Sports

This will be topical on a school sports day and also when there is a marathon, or any big sporting occasion, in your area. You may even want to use it when Commonwealth, or Olympic, Games are due!

Aim

To appreciate the qualities of competitive sports.

Props

Make a display of notices about sports events in your school or town. Arrange any trophies you are able to borrow, with appropriate equipment, to make an attractive setting for your assembly.

Reading

In the Old Testament, Ecclesiastes, Chapter 9, verse 11, gives an unusual but good view of a race. You may prefer to choose a poem about a sporting occasion — there are many. Ask your English teacher or librarian to help you select one.

Facts

● *Find out from books* Read in a reference book all you can find about the Olympic Games. Discover why the laurel wreath was used to crown winners in the first games, and all you can unearth about the medals awarded to modern competitors.

Contact your nearest Sports Council Office for leaflets and information. The more you tell them of your particular needs, the more useful will be the information they supply. Don't forget the stamped envelope! If your local Sports Council is unable to help, try the Information Office of the Sports Council in London, 16 Upper Woburn Place, London WC1H 0QP.

● *Find out from people* Ask a pupil who competes at county or national level what they gain from sport on that level. If you have a well-known sporting personality in your area, you might persuade them to write a little about their life, or even come to talk about their sport. Many such people are very generous about giving time to schools.

Presentation

1. It is possible that two of your fellow-students who take opposing views about sports would be willing to discuss the subject in a dialogue, with yourself as chairperson. For example, someone who hates sport and regrets its place in school life could debate this with a team captain who is enthusiastic about the game.

2. You could give a brief survey of the founding of the Olympic tradition, looking at the Greek games founded in 776 BC and their re-introduction in 1896. It will be easy to discover from books, the venues and dates of modern games, and a survey of relevant issues of national newspapers at your reference library will give you a choice of fascinating stories to quote.

3. You may prefer to discard the Olympic theme and rely on your own experience of sport as part of school life or leisure activity. Whichever line you take, the emphasis should be on the importance of taking part, not just on being first.

    The recent fashion for charity-sport gives a good opportunity to say that sometimes athletes compete not for personal gain or honour, but to help others. The 1985 London marathon raised about four million pounds for charity. (Does your school have a charity-run or similar event you could quote?) Emphasise that all this is not as serious and high-minded as it sounds — it's meant to be fun! Jimmy Savile, some of whose thoughts you can read in the assembly on death (no. 5) is a TV personality who has completed twenty-six marathons. In the last he raised £100,000 for the disabled; he used a portable telephone to speak with his sister in Australia as he ran.

    Many competitors in the London marathon make it a fun-run, wearing fancy dress and delighting the crowds with their antics, but the most memorable competitors, for many of the crowd, are those who run with almost incredible handicaps. Like the blind girl, the first totally blind woman to attempt the race, who was linked to another runner, her 'eyes', and who was greeted joyfully by her guide-dog as she passed the tape.

    No laurel wreath, no winner's medal, awaited one young man as he steered his wheelchair to the finish; he had artificial hands and legs, but the look of achievement on his face said it all.

    What would they say, these athletes, dedicated runners, housewives, people with multiple disabilities, if asked why they compete like this, not only in London but around the world? Most of them would talk about determination, and practice, about keeping going when breath is short and muscles ache. They'd tell you of the sheer thrill of completing the course, of staying to the finish . . . not for a medal, but for the achievement of getting to the tape.

Conclusion

For some of us, sports are the best thing about school. To others games are a nightmare, but perhaps if we all thought less about beating others and more about getting the best from ourselves, we'd all benefit. This could be true of many other things besides sport . . . think about it.

33
Superstitions

Many people think a Friday 13th is an unlucky day so you could use this then, or at any other time.

Aim

To show the foolishness of superstition.

Props

A ladder. A pot of red paint, on a hook, and a paintbursh. A sling.

Facts

● *Find out from books* Read about superstitions and their origins in a reference or non-fiction book. Peter Maining, *Superstitions* (Sidgwick & Jackson, 1979) is excellent but there are many others.

● *Find out from people* Ask your family and friends about their 'pet' superstitions — note any that are unusual!

Presentation

You may like to introduce this subject by quoting some of the superstitions you have discovered from reading or from friends. It would be interesting if everyone in turn told of a different superstition — you might find the few who were totally free from such fears!

Alternatively, with a little preparation, you could present something like the following playlet, using your own ideas.

Five pupils, or more, will be needed. One carries a ladder, which he mounts, hanging the pot of paint on a rung. He then produces a brush, whistling as he dips it in the paint. Another pupil walks under the ladder, and red splashes appear on his sleeve. The third pupil comes on from the other side and points to the red 'paint' on the jacket.

3 What have you been up to, is it blood?

2 No, of course it's not blood. I only walked under that ladder — and I got splashed!

3 What do you expect, doing a mad thing like that, especially today.

Pupil 4 enters, running . . .

4 Gosh, I was nearly late! A button came off my jeans and Mum insisted on sewing it on, while I was wearing them . . . of course, I had to wait until she'd gone to work, then change them. Couldn't have worn them — especially today!

2 Will somebody tell me what's so special about today?

3 & 4 It's Friday the thirteenth!

1 (*From ladder.*) You have to be extra careful today or terrible things will happen

to you. Look what happens if thirteen people sit together at a table . . . a disaster is sure to follow. The Romans believed that, so it must be true!

3 That's right. My Dad says if thirteen people sit down together, the last one to get up from the table dies in a year.

4 Well, I'll be late for school if I don't get going. They say it's unlucky to walk under a ladder, unless you spit on your shoe first, then go straight under, and don't look back! (*Spits on shoe and walks under ladder.*)

3 My Gran says you can walk under a ladder if you keep silent afterwards until you've seen a four-legged animal. Keep your fingers crossed that I'll see a black cat soon, then I'll be lucky. . . . (*Walks under.*)

2 It will be lucky for me if you don't. . . . I could do without your chatter — especially when it's all this superstitious nonsense.

Beyond the ladder, 2 and 3 meet pupil 5, coming towards them with arm in a sling. 3 holds lips together with fingers in case tempted to speak.

2 What's up with you then? Fighting again?

5 No, I got knocked down by a motor-bike. I only stepped into the road to avoid going under a ladder. Didn't want any bad luck, did I?

Conclusion

Most of us are superstitious about something. If we discover the reason for these apparently dangerous things or actions we often find that our fear is quite unreasonable.

34
Teamwork
Sir Ranulph Fiennes, DSO

Topical for school team or other joint effort occasions.

Aim

To show how much individuals can do when they work together.

Props

A stick about 60 cm long and a bundle of the same kind of sticks, bound tightly together.

Facts

● *Find out from books* Read how teams of people accomplished heroic or useful feats that could not have succeeded if done by individuals. *To the Ends of the Earth* by Ranulph Fiennes is a good book (Hodder and Stoughton paperback).

● *Find out from people* Think of a local group working for a charity, and talk to one of its officers. Or go to the Fire Station and ask about teamwork there. If you have a local football team, ask to interview the manager and hear his views on teamwork. Perhaps the captain of your school games or gymnastic teams will say a little about teamwork at school.

Readings

You may like to read one of the accounts of Jesus picking his team — the apostles — from a modern version of the New Testament (Matthew 4, verses 18-22); or read the list of Expedition Team members given in Appendix One of Ranulph Fiennes, *To the Ends of the Earth.*

Music

If you are featuring a football team, they may have a theme song you can play, e.g. 'The Saints Go Marching' for Southampton Football Team. . . .

Presentation

Speak about your chosen type of team . . . quote its leader on how much can be accomplished when people work together. Consider what happens to teams when one person drops out, or doesn't pull their weight.

If you have read Sir Ranulph Fiennes' book, *To the Ends of the Earth,* you will be impressed by the number of people who were backing up the expedition, yet only two men actually made the supreme effort of Trans-globing. It seems strange that until February 1972, nobody had planned to go round the world from North to South and back again. Sir Ranulph Fiennes, inspired by his wife, decided to make

E

the attempt. It would mean covering thousands of miles from seas of ice to deserts, and Sir Ran knew that the hardships would be many and long-lasting.

Encouraged by the Prince of Wales, and supported by many sponsors, the adventure passed from planning to performance. It all sounds very easy. In fact, it took from September 1979 to August 1982 to go round the world from Britain to the South Pole, on to the North Pole and home again. Two men made the whole of the epic treck, but the back-up team was all-important. Ran's wife, Virginia, managed the communications and commanded bases, three men flew and serviced the aircraft, two more maintained the UK radio base . . . the list of helpers seems endless. Behind them stood the crew of the ice-breaker they needed for polar seas and the many committees which helped and advised. Even Bothie, the Fiennes' little dog, played his part in the success of the adventure, keeping up spirits and providing companionship.

The trip was not just to achieve a first by going round the world from pole to pole; much useful scientific research was undertaken and many British products were exported as a result of exhibitions held along the way.

But all this was not possible for one man alone . . . it was being part of a team that brought success, as the acknowledgements in Sir Ran's account prove. . . .

(You may find that you are using another example from your own research to demonstrate team spirit, but a practical illustration may be useful as a flourish at the end. . . .)

Take one stick and break it, snapping it as you apply pressure at the end. Then show your bundle of sticks and ask someone to break it, as you have broken the single stick. It will prove impossible. . . . Perhaps you have proved that unity is strength. . . .

Conclusion

Few of us can be completely independent and go-it-alone. People working together often have more strength than each one would have, working alone.

35
Thankyou

This would be topical when a teacher is leaving the school, or when pupils are ending their school lives.

Aim

To examine ways of being thankful, and reasons for gratitude.

Reading

You may like to use Luke chapter 17, verses 11-18.

Facts

● *Find out from people* Write to a national or local charity to find out if they are ever thanked. Ask a doctor, nurse or bank manager if patients or customers every thank them. Enquire from your friends how many in their class give their teacher a thankyou card or gift at Christmas or end of term.

Music

You may find some appropriate music on tape, like: 'Thankyou for waking me this morning'; or 'Thankyou very much for the Aintree iron'.

Presentation

Make a collection of graces or thankyou prayers. Some families still say grace before meals. Perhaps different pupils could quote their own or use these:

a. For what we are about to receive, accept our thanks. Amen.

b. Some ha' meat and canna eat, and some can eat, but want it. But we ha' meat and we can eat, so let the Lord be thankit.

c. Ta Pa. Amen.

These are three different ways of saying thankyou, coming from different parts of the world. Pupils from different faiths may have their own ways of saying thankyou to enrich this assembly.

Perhaps you think it's very old-fashioned and boring for people to give thanks out loud before they eat. In fact, you may be one of the many people who find it unnecessary or embarrassing to say thankyou to anyone, ever. Or perhaps you feel that the way most of us say thankyou is too formal and doesn't mean very much.

There are many ways in which we say thankyou . . . verbally, by letter or card, with a gift, or even a kiss. Take clapping. This is a traditional way for a group of people to express their pleasure and gratitude to someone who has served them, or performed for them. After a concert or a play, we bang our hands together so that the performers know we enjoyed the gig or show . . . we are saying thankyou.

Sometimes, even clapping is not enough. Young Andrew Jonathan was taken to a London Theatre for the first time to see 'Rockets in Ursa Major'. He was much younger than anyone here and he'd never seen anything like this play. Before this, his experience of drama had been on the small screen or at school performances. He was spell-bound, hardly even able to eat an icecream in the interval. At the end, when the actors stepped forward to take their bow, the audience clapped. Not the polite applause you sometimes hear, but a long and hearty hand-banging from all round the house. Everyone was clapping. Everyone was smiling.

Not Andrew Jonathan.

Andrew was applauding as wildly as everyone else but he was also shouting. He was standing on his seat, bellowing at the top of his voice, and becuase he was in the front row and like most boys had a great shout, the actors actually heard his words. He was shouting,

'Thankyou very much . . . that was ace!'

Inevitably, parents being what they are, Andrew was hurriedly pulled from his perch and half smothered by a red-faced mother and an angry father. Even his twin brother looked offended by the outburst. But the cast was delighted. It's not every day that a member of the audience stands on the seat of the Mermaid Theatre in London, or any other place of entertainment for that matter, and shouts Thankyou!

Maybe we should all be doing just that. Not standing on seats, of course, but saying thankyou as if we really mean it. You can think up your own ways of saying thankyou . . . you will know the people you'd want to say it to. Teachers: when schooldays are long past most of us realise too late what a lot we owe them. Parents: we all take them for granted. Sometimes, even when it's not Dad's birthday or Mother's Day, a son or daughter says a special thankyou to the one who's made life good for them.

How about the postman, the bus driver, the girl who serves at the chip shop? (If this is a leaving-assembly, you'll want to make special mention here about the qualities of a teacher, or of the school, that deserve thanks.)

Conclusion

People with a real faith will want to acknowledge that their first thanks should go to

God, by whatever name they know him. Each one of us could make a long list of the people who have helped us be the way we are, giving us opportunities, caring in many ways. A day could come-alive for many people if we remembered to say thankyou — and said it as if we meant it.

36
Time
New Year

New Year is celebrated at different times by various communities. This assembly would be suitable for many dates, or for the times of year when clocks are changed to adjust for the coming of summer or winter.

Aim

To look at time, the way we use or misuse it, particularly in the light of New Year with its fresh start.

Props

Make a long banner, which says Happy New Year, perhaps with help from the art department. If you can repeat this phrase in several languages the effect would be heightened.

Facts

● *Find out from books* Read the SHAP Calendar of Religious Festivals. From Shap Working Party, 7 Alderbrook Rd., Solihull B91 1NH. This lists the New Year celebrations of many different faiths. For example, you will discover that the Jewish New Year's Day is in September while the Japanese celebrate New Year in January, with festivities for up to three days and the first visit of the year to the local Shinto shrines.

● *Find out from people* Ask people from a culture different from your own about their New Year festivities. If you can find nobody at school who can help from their experience, try the staff of a Chinese or Indian restaurant. The difference in the celebrations of New Year even within the British Isles is worth noting. Leaders at your nearest centres of worship, such as temples, synagogues, mosques, will be glad to inform you about their New Year customs and celebrations.

Presentation

1. If you are offering a straightforward assembly it may be a good idea to examine in some detail the concept of New Year. While this is a fixed date in Western calendars, for many people it is a moveable feast, determined by the phase of the moon or other factors. Whatever the date, for most societies the New Year signals a fresh start; some go to great lengths to make sure that everything they use is, in fact, really clean and fresh. New Year becomes a time for new resolutions, decisions to be more hardworking, honest, kind and so on. You may find a few volunteers who will be prepared to talk about their own New Year resolutions, and the plans they make to ensure these are kept through the year.

2. If there are people at school who are celebrating New Year on a date other than early January, this is an ideal chance to focus on this fresh start in another month. A review of their celebrations would be enlightening and probably entertaining. A Chinese dragon could be a sensation at school . . . perhaps your art department would be persuaded to make one, if given sufficient notice.

3. The change from summertime to wintertime, or vice versa, when we alter our clocks and watches to regulate the daylight hours calls for a different consideration of time. This is the opportunity to look at the way we talk of gaining or losing an hour and prompts thoughts on our use of time. If you have time to spare you could adapt the following playlet. . . .

Preparations

Arrange for a student with a good loud voice, and some acting ability, to be near the back of the room, with a portable typewriter. Organise two other pupils to make interruptions, strictly according to plan! Either play some suitable music which indicates time, or have two pupils reading Ecclesiastes chapter 3, verses 1-8 from the Living Bible as a dialogue, taking alternate verses.

As reading or music ends, the person with the typewriter interrupts, from the back.

Student *(talking loudly as he or she walks forward and dumps the typewriter on table or desk)* All this talk about time . . . (New Year or summer-winter time) I'll tell you what I think . . . it's time we killed Qwerty! He's had his day . . . it's time Qwerty was dead!

Voice 1 Who is Qwerty?

2 What's Qwerty done?

1 Who are you, anyway?

Student I'm a typist. I sit all day long, typing letters for my boss. Minutes of meetings, reports, info-sheets, endlessly tapping the keys. I've even got an electronic machine at the office but I still have to tap out the letters.

Voice 1 Now we know who you are and what you do, but who is Qwerty?

2 What's he done?

Student Qwerty is the way letters are arranged on the top line of a typewriter keyboard . . . you know, Q W E R T Y and so on. It's called the Qwerty plan.

Voice 1 Well?

2 So what?

Student Now some guy has invented a new plan for typewriter symbols. He says it would save me hours every day. In fact, I read that a typist could save twelve finger miles a year. Isn't that something? I think Qwerty is old-fashioned. He doesn't fit in this modern technological age. . . . He should be dead!

Voice 1 Twelve finger miles sounds like a lot of time!

2 If Qwerty dies, what will you do with the time you save?

Student It's my time anyway, I can save it or spend it, I can waste it if I choose.

Conclusion

Maybe this is a good time to consider how we use the minutes, hours, days of this New Year . . . of the rest of our life. So often we say . . . 'Sorry, I can't help, I've no time' or 'I didn't come to support the team . . . I'd no time'. Isn't it time we said, 'Yes, I'll find the time' . . . stop wasting the minutes that run into hours.

Sadly, when we've missed opportunities we long to say with Shakespeare, 'O call back yesterday, bid time return!' But that unforgiving minute that Kipling wrote about will not return.

Today could be the right day to think of Stephen Grellet's words: 'I expect to pass through this world but once; any good thing therefore that I can do, or any kindness that I can show to any fellow creature, let me do it now, let me not defer or neglect it, for I shall not pass this way again.'

⊳ A,T

37
Two kinds of courage
Louis Pasteur and Jean Baptiste Jupille

This could be topical in the Child of Courage Award week.

Aim

To consider the instant courage of Jean Baptiste Jupille in defending his friends from physical danger and the courage of Louis Pasteur in risking his reputation to save the boy.

Props

A rabies warning poster, obtainable from your nearest airport or harbour. If you live too far from these, write to HMSO.

Facts

● *Find out from books* Read about rabies and its effects on victims. Study the life of Louis Pasteur in a biography or reference book.

● *Find out from people* Most towns and many villages have a statue or memorial. It may be in the parish church. Choose a statue which you feel represents courage of some kind. Then ask people you know, or passers-by, what the person commemorated means to them.

Music

Some French music might be useful here. Ask your A/V department if they have a suitable tape you could use.

Presentation

Read out the basic warning on the rabies poster and describe the symptoms of this terrible disease. Underline the fact that rabies is kept from spreading by strict laws on the transfer of animals.

Just over a hundred years ago a bite from a rabies infected animal almost certainly meant an agonising death. Louis Pasteur, a French scientist, already well known for his outstanding research, was appalled by the effects a bite from a mad dog had on its victims. He began to experiment, even risking his own life to suck a few drops of the deadly saliva from the jaws of a rabid dog which was strapped to a bench. After some years of research, he felt it was time to try the vaccine he had developed on a human being. The big question was whether the injection, if given after a bite, would prevent the dread disease. While he was debating whether to give himself rabies and then try to stop the course of the disease in his own body, two boys in different parts of France were bitten by rabid dogs.

F

The first, Joseph Meister, was only nine years old. It was 6 July 1888. Louis looked at the child's fourteen wounds and faced the risks involved in treatment. Since the symptoms develop long after a bite, it was possible that Joseph would be lucky and escape the disease. It was also possible that he was already infected and doomed to die. . . .

Joseph and his mother were given lodgings in Paris and every day for a fortnight the child was given a daily injection of the anti-rabies serum. To Louis the days were endless, as he watched Joseph playing and knew that he could either have hastened his death, or prevented a tragedy. . . . While the boy slept peacefully at night, the scientist lived through hours of doubt and fear. At the end of fourteen days the child returned home, safe and happy, probably the first person in the world to be given anti-rabies serum.

In October that same year, 1888, a boy from Villers-Farlay, in the Jura mountains, close to Louis' own childhood home, nearly died for his friends. A fourteen-year old shepherd boy, Jean Baptiste Jupille, was playing with five others. A mad dog attacked them, but Jean grabbed his whip and fought to defend his friends. Heedless of the pain from bites and scratches, the boy finally wound his whip round the dog's jaws and killed it with a blow from his heavy clog.

Six days after the fight, Jean reached Louis Pasteur's laboratory, and a course of anti-rabies injections began at once, with total success. Jean not only received a prize for his courage — a statue of him was erected in the courtyard of the Pasteur Institute in Paris.

Conclusion

Courage is impossible to measure. It may take the form of unpremeditated action like Jean's or it may be long-term dedication like Louis Pasteur. But courage should always be honoured, whether by a statue — like Jean's, or possibly one in your area — or in the hearts and memories of people who know that the world would be much worse without the bravery of men, women . . . and children.

38
Water

This will be topical in time of drought, or unusually heavy rainfall, or flooding. It could also be used if your district is affected by a strike of water-workers.

Aim

To foster awareness of something we take for granted. Water is under-rated in some parts of the world, while thousands die for its lack in other areas.

Props

A tumbler each of milk and water. Individual size cans and bottles of drinks like Coke, squash, etc. Also a watch with a second hand or digital seconds.

Posters showing water in many forms . . . rivers, seas, rain, wells. . . .

Music

There are many tapes featuring water; your media department may have recordings of water as sound effects or your teacher may help you make a short recording of your own watery sounds — a tap running or hands swishing water in a bowl.

Reading

Look up references to water in a bible or some other scripture, or ask the librarian to help you find a good poem or prose passage on this.

Facts

● *Find out from books* See A. & D. Lucas, *Focus on Water* (Methuens Childrens Books, 1976); J. Sowry, *Water* (Priory Press, 1977). Excellent source material will be found in *Our Water* (National Water Council, 1 Queen Anne's Gate, London SW1H 9BT): this contains a list of other publications, and of films on the subject. You may find that the divisional headquarters of the local Water Authority will give or sell you leaflets, posters, etc. Contact first by phone and follow with a letter if necessary.

Write to one of the national aid agencies, like Oxfam or Christian Aid (addresses at back) for anything they have on drought or water supply.

● *Find out from people* Ask a farmer or gardener how much water affects his livelihood. Water has much religious significance. How is it used in baptism and initiation rites? You may know people who can tell you.

Presentation

You will need to ask for complete silence as you start an experiment. Asking pupils with watches to time the silent minute is one way to ensure quiet! Say that during the minute you will point, every three seconds, at one of your group, who will then walk quickly and quietly to stand behind you. When you have twenty 'volunteers' your minute should be up. . . .

Explain that during the sixty seconds just passed, twenty children in the world will have died from illnesses related to deficient water and sanitation. . . .

Before your twenty go back to their places, ask them to take a drink from the array before you. It is probable that the well-known cans and cartons will be claimed first. The water is likely to be the last drink accepted, and you should then have several pupils who have been left with nothing to drink.

Your helpers can return to their places while you share some of the facts you have gleaned from your reading and research.

Drought means empty rivers and wells, dead cattle, thirst and hunger and dirt. Drought means malnutrition for one child in two. Drought means a depressed area, however hard the people work, whatever they do.

In Africa alone twenty-five countries are affected by drought yet the rich countries of the world take water for granted. Imagine a day without any water. How will you keep clean and healthy? Can you cook without water? How many activities in your school and home depend on the use of water?

Now that we have seen how necessary water is to our daily lives we begin to appreciate what drought really means. What can we do to help? Not surprisingly, but little known, the very workers who make it possible for people in Britain to have fresh water in their homes, are helping those in other lands who suffer from drought. As long ago as 1981 the British Water Industry started Water Aid to help other countries in the nineteen eighties.

Water Aid tries to make British water users aware of the needs of people in the poor parts of the world. It also makes grants to help provide basic needs in deprived areas, so that water reaches health centres and places where it is most urgently needed.

In one Midlands town, very much depressed by unemployment and local problems, a water worker won a Christmas turkey when he had already bought one for his family. The next day he took the bird to work, where it was raffled and the cash raised was sent to Water Aid. Water can't be exported like food, but the tools and the expertise to make barren land productive can be provided.

Conclusion

Human beings round the world have very few things in common. The need for water is one of these. If we are aware enough, if we care enough, maybe we will live to see a time when not a single child dies from lack of water.

39
What's in a name?

This will be topical if your school has a distinctive name and you use this assembly for the start of a new academic year, to introduce the school to new pupils. It will also be topical if a royal, or otherwise well-known child, has just been named.

Aim

To feature our fore-names; the way they are chosen by different cultural groups.

Reading

Quotations from the naming ceremonies of different faiths. The baptismal service of the Church of England could be one, but try to get extracts from other religious ceremonies, if only a few words. For suggestions, see below and also check booklist at back. 'Milestones' by C. Collinson and C. Miller (E. Arnold) is very explicit.

Facts

● *Find out from books* Discover from a book on comparative religion how names are chosen by different groups. Read about the ritual which attends the naming of a child. (See General Booklist.)

● *Find out from people* Ask your parents why they chose your name. Choose a few people in your group who have unusual names and ask about these. If they are willing, get them in your assembly to say a few words about the name and its origin. Visit a naming ceremony at your local temple or mosque or ask at a nearby church if you may attend a baptismal service.

Presentation

Have you ever thought what life would be like if we had no names? Perhaps we would have numbers, like cars, to identify us. Imagine your teacher reading the register like this . . . . (Ask a teacher to read a list of car numbers you have provided:

A 764 GUE
SUY 849 B
FNO 754 T. . . .)

It might be simpler if we were numbered like books in the school library. . . . (The teacher could call a register like this:

007.9824
021.76843
332.87649. . . .)

You can probably invent many other ways of identifying yourselves. In the end it's likely that you'll consider that the identification provided by our names is the best. One of the great advantages is that names are personal, especially first names.

Our family names are inherited, and sometimes have great traditions behind them, but our forenames are all our own. (At this point you may ask your volunteers with unusual names to say them aloud and explain in a few words about why their parents chose them.)

Most royal names are rooted in history, like John, Edward, Elizabeth and George. But many monarchs are known by names which were not the first choice when they were babies. Queen Victoria was baptised Alexandra Victoria and King George VI was Albert, and known to his family as Bertie all his life. In our generation some of the royal family have dared to be different — Princess Anne's daughter is called Zara, a very new name for a grandchild of a Queen.

It's not only royals who prefer other names to those chosen by their parents. Imagine a boy called Marion! You know all about Marion Morris — he was probably one of the best-known men in the world. It's just that you know him by his chosen name of John Wayne. He would probably never have become a strong-man film star if he'd kept his given name of Marion.

Most faiths have a very special ceremony when a child is named, and many believers choose a child's name with great care. A Hindu baby will be given a name selected from several which the priest has proposed after preparing a horoscope for the child. (Describe the Hindu naming ceremony, if any of this faith are present.)

Jews frequently choose very traditional names for their children: the Hebrew name for the baby is announced at the appropriate ceremony for a new-born child.

For a boy-child, Muslims usually choose one of the ninety-nine names by which they know Allah. The actual decision is often left to a senior member of the family, perhaps a grandfather. Sons and daughters are frequently called after a great Muslim of history. One of the more social effects of a Muslim naming ceremony benefits the poor: the child's head is shaved and the value in gold or silver of the weight of hair is given to charity. (If Muslims are present, expand on their naming ritual.)

Sikhs consult their holy book, the *Guru Granth Sahib,* when naming their children. The name is chosen using the first letter of the first word read and the last letter of the last word read. The chosen name is then announced, together with the traditional names, Singh for a boy and Kaur for a girl. (If Sikhs are at the assembly, enlarge on their naming ceremony.)

Most Christians have a service of infant baptism to name a child, but some believe in adult baptism and so they have a ceremony of dedication in which the child is named and offered to God.

In the traditional baptism service the names have already been decided by the parents. Some choose traditional Christian names, like the names of the saints. Others are influenced by family history or by names that are popular at the time. While some parents regard the public baptism as a matter of form, the sincere believers feel that it is a chance to offer their child to God and to promise to bring him or her up in the Christian faith. (You may quote some of the baptismal service here.)

Conclusion

Whatever has influenced the choice of our names, and regardless of the type of ceremony performed, there is no doubt that the rite of naming a child has great significance. Today, then, is a time to be thankful that we are all individuals . . . not numbers like cars or books, but people with different personalities and our own special names.

40

Words

This assembly will be topical if used at the Christian festival of Whitsun (Pentecost). Alternatively, it may be used at anytime to underline the way we all use words.

Aim

To look at the meaning behind many of the words we say casually.

Reading

If using the Christian aspect: Acts 2, verses 1-3 from the Good News Bible, or some other version.

Props

Make a pile of all the dictionaries you can gather. Your school librarian may lend you multi-volume works and colourful modern books.

Facts

● *Find out from books* Choose a few key words and find alternative ways of expressing their meaning. Collins' Thesaurus will give you many different ways of using one word or phrase. Ask several members of your group to say these alternatives when required.

● *Find out from people* Ask people from different backgrounds how they greet each other first thing in the morning, or after an absence.

Presentation

Words! If today's lessons in school were to be broadcast, the BBC would expect us to get through about one hundred and fifty words a minute. . . . (You could estimate the length of lessons in your school day and arrive at a total of words used by one class in a day. Multiply this by the forms in your school and you should have a staggering number of words for the day.)

Many of the words we use most casually have meanings hidden so deep that they are almost forgotten. Take *goodbye* . . . it really means 'God be with you!' yet few of us think of God when we say Goodbye. In many other languages, the words for greeting or parting involve God in some way. Muslims will say, *Assalamo Alaikum* which means 'peace be with you'. . . . Hindus greet each other with *Namaste* . . . 'I bow to you'. Sikhs also use a greeting that refers to their faith. *Sat Sri Akal, Ji* means 'truth is eternal' . . . an undisputed basis of their belief. Jews have the phrase *Shalom* which invokes the peace of God.

We have become so used to words, even of greeting and parting, that we use them very lightly, yet we'd be lost without them! Take your breakfast this morning . . . was it a snap-crackle-pop cereal or lip-licking bacon and egg? Have you just enjoyed a good weekend, a great break, or even a super time? (This could be the opportunity to ask your volunteers to read the alternatives from the Thesaurus for the chosen words.)

Most things are pretty easy to describe. Meals and holidays, lessons and houses have ready words in any language. Problems come when situations arise for which no words are adequate. How do you explain the horror that strikes you when your mind goes blank as you stare at an exam paper? How do you describe your real feelings when you fall in love? Where are the words to tell a child that a dearly loved grandparent has died?

Faced with the last problem, a young mother remembered that one enthusiasm her father had shared with her little boy was a love of trains. The child had vivid memories of hours he'd spent at the railway terminus, watching the trains arrive. Pulling in to rest at the buffers, the engines had seemed to be at home after a long, eventful journey. So when the boy asked how his grandfather died, his mother told him it was like a train reaching its destination, and the child understood.

The friends of Jesus Christ had this problem of finding the right words to describe what happened to them at Pentecost. When the Holy Spirit came to them in the upper room, these ordinary men needed to translate the experience into words. Like the mother with her son, they chose familiar things to describe a special experience. So they talked of tongues of fire and a mighty wind. Fire that warmed them, spread a glow. Wind that guided their fishing boats with unseen power. This experience, so hard to describe, made them new people; men and women whose lives had a warmth and a drive unknown before.

Conclusion

However we describe God, whether we really acknowledge him or not, he is always present with us. . . . Present in our greetings, with his peace. Present in our goodbyes. . . . We may not have the words to explain his presence — some things are beyond words.

Reference Booklist

This is a short list of reference books recommended for the school library, as resources for assembly material. If your school can afford only one reference work, the *World Book Encyclopedia* may be the best choice, as it has information on most of the topics covered in these assemblies.

Children's Britannica (Encyclopedia Britannica, 1985)
Collins Modern Encyclopedia in Colour (Collins, 1977)
Collins New World Thesaurus (Collins, 1979)
Encyclopedia of Dates and Events (Hodder & Stoughton, 1979)
Everyman's Factfinder (Dent, 1982)
Hamlyn Dictionary of Dates and Anniversaries (Hamlyn, 1979)
Illustrated Encyclopedia of Science and the Future (Marshall Cavendish, 1983)
The World's Religions: Lion Handbook (Lion, 1982)
New Oxford Illustrated Dictionary (Bay Books, with Oxford University Press, 1978)
J. B. Noss, *Man's Religions* (Macmillan, 1984)
Pears Cyclopedia (Pelham Books, 1984-5)
Penguin Dictionary of Religions (Penguin, 1984)
Penguin Dictionary of the Twentieth Century 1900-1982 (Penguin, 1983)
Readers' Digest Book of Facts (Macmillan, 1985)
B. Schofield, *Events in Britain* (Blandford Press, 19   )
Social Services, Guide to the (Family Welfare Association, 1985)
Whitaker's Almanac (1984)
Peter D. Bishop, *Words in World's Religions* (SCM Press, 1979)
World Book Encyclopedia (World Books, 1983)

General Booklist

Books marked with an asterisk* contain passages from the world's scriptures in a form suitable for reading out loud.

All the books listed below were available in public libraries in the UK in 1985.

Bahree, P., *The Hindu World* (Macdonald, 1982)

*Bhagavad Gita, The, a verse translation by G. Parrinder (Sheldon Press) Hindu

*Bible, The: there are many modern versions which read well. *Good News Bible* (Collins) and *The Living Bible For Young People* (Kingsway, 1983) are two of many.

**Bishop, P., *Words in World Religions* (SCM Press, 1979)

Bloom, L., *To Heaven with Scribes and Pharisees: the Jewish Path to God* (Darton, Longman and Todd, 1975)

Bowker, J., *Words of Faith: Religious Belief and Practice in Britain Today* (BBC Publications, 1983)

**Butler, D.G., *Rejoicing in our Midst* (Edward Arnold, 1980)

**Cole, W.O. and Piara Singh Sambhi, *The Sikhs* (Routledge and Kegan Paul, 1978)

**Davies, R., *The Holy Books* (Longman, 1981)

Fyson, N.L., *Multi-Ethnic Britian* (Batsford, 1984)

Green, V.J., *Festivals and Saints' Days* (Blandford Press, 1983)

**Guru Nanak, *Sayings*, prepared by Dr Harnam Singh Shan, Sikh

**Herod, F.G., *What Men Believe* (Methuen) 1975

*The Hindu Tradition (Argus Publications, 1979)

*Kaballah, part of the Hebrew Bible (Open Court Publications, 1977) Jewish

*Koran, The, translated with notes by N.J. Dawood (Penguin, 1976) Muslim. See also, *The Qur'an*

Oliver, I.P., *Buddhism in Britain* (Rider and Company, 1979)

Palmer, M. and Bisset, E., *Worlds of Difference* (Blackie and World Wildlife Fund, 1985)

**Parrinder, G., *Worship in the World's Religions* (Sheldon Press, 1979)

**Prickett, J., *Death* (Living Faiths, Lutterworth, 1980)

*Qur'an, The, Basic Teachings, (The Islamic Foundation, Leicester)

**Talib, G.S., *Selections from the Holy Granth* (Vikas, India)

*Torah, The, Way of the, Introduction to Judaism (J. Neusner, Duxbury, 1979) Jewish

*Vedas, Wisdom of the (Theosophical Publishing House, 1973) Hindu scriptures

**Whiting, J.R.S., *Religions of Man* (Stanley Thornes, 1983)

Wigley, B., *Paths to Faith* (Longman, 1970)

Research Booklist

Suggestions for books to refer to for particular topics

This is not a comprehensive list for each topic, but a survey guide drawn up by Lesley Hart, reference librarian at Kidderminster Public Library, to show you how to research topics. Topics given in brackets suggest other headings to use for looking up particular subjects.

Badges   Wilkinson, F., *Badges of the British Army* 1820-1980
                           Arms and Armour, 1982
Barbed Wire *World Book Encyclopedia*
(Amnesty International)
Blood donors *World Book Encyclopedia*
Buddhism *World Book Encyclopedia*
Cheshire, Leonard *Who's Who* 1984
Commonwealth Games   Arlott, J., *Oxford Companion to Sports and Games* (Oxford University Press 1975)
Deafness *World Book Encyclopedia*
                 Social Services Yearbook for the current year
Death *International Encyclopedia of the Social Sciences* (Macmillan 1968)
Diamond Sutra   Parrinder, G., *A Dictionary of Non-Christian Religions* (Hulton 1971)
Drugs *International Encyclopedia of the Social Sciences* (op. cit.)
Donors *World Book Encyclopedia*
Dustbins *World Book Encyclopedia*
(Waste Disposal)
Easter *Standard Dictionary of Folklore* (Funk and Wagnall, 1949)
Eggs *World Book Encyclopedia*
Envelope *World Book Encyclopedia*
Equality *World Book Encyclopedia*
Equinox *World Book Encyclopedia*
Fair trading *International Encyclopedia of the Social Sciences*
Fiennes, Sir Ranulph *Who's Who* 1984
Fingerprints *World Book Encyclopedia*
(Crime) *Annual Abstract of Statistics*
Games   Arlott, J., *Oxford Companion to Sports and Games* (Oxford University Press)
Harvest *Standard Dictionary of Folklore* (Funk and Wagnall)
Highway Code *The Highway Code*
Hill, Sir Rowland *Dictionary of National Biography*
Honesty   Hastings, J., *Encyclopedia of Religion and Ethics* (Clark, 1908)
King, Martin Luther *World Book Encyclopedia*

Mine rescue *World Book Encyclopedia* (Mining)

Names   Withycombe, E.G., *Oxford Dictionary of English Christian Names*, (Oxford University Press, 1977)

Reaney, P.H., *A Dictionary of British Surnames* (Routledge and Kegan Paul, 1976)

Ekwall, *Oxford Dictionary of English place-names* (Oxford University Press 1960)

News   Keesing's Contemporary Archives

Ceefax/Oracle

Local and National Newspapers

New Year *World Book Encyclopedia*

Olympic Games *Guinness Book of Olympic Facts and Feats* (Guinness 1983)

Pentecost *Oxford Dictionary of the Christian Church* (Oxford University Press)

Post Office Post Code Directories

Telephone Directories

Post Office Guide

Racial Equality *International Encyclopedia of the Social Sciences*

Red Cross *Charities Digest* for the current year

Rescue — mines

— at sea *World Book Encyclopedia*

RNID *Charities Digest* for the current year

Royal Commonwealth Society for the Blind *Charities Digest* for the current year

RNLI *Charities Digest* for the current year

Rubbish *World Book Encyclopedia*

Samaritans *Charities Digest* for the current year

Savile, Jimmy *Who's Who* 1984

Shipwreck *World Book Encyclopedia*

Spare-part surgery *World Book Encyclopedia*

Special offers *Shopping by Post for Gardners* (Exley 1980)

Exchange & Mart

Sport   Arlott, J., *Oxford Companion to Sports and Games* (Oxford University Press)

Superstitions   Radford, E. & M. A., *Encyclopedia of Superstitions* (Hutchinson 1961)

Sutra   Parrinder, G., *A Dictionary of Non-Christian Religions*

Teamwork *Rules of the Game* (Paddington Press 1974)

Text books *World Book Encyclopedia*

Thanks (Thanksgiving day) *World Book Encyclopedia*

Time *World Book Encyclopedia*

Transplant *World Book Encyclopedia*

Varah, Chad *Who's Who* 1984

Water *World Book Encyclopedia*

Whitsun *Standard Dictionary of Folklore* (Funk and Wagnall)

Wilson, John *Who's Who* 1984

Words *Chamber's 20th Century Dictionary*

Rogets' Thesaurus

Work *The Job Book 1985* (Careers Resource Advisory Council 1984)

Annual Careers Guide (Careers Resource Advisory Council)

Addresses of Organisations in the United Kingdom

The following UK organisations have consented to supply information if you write and ask for help. Please don't forget to include adequate postage to cover their reply to you.

Amnesty International, 8 Southampton St, London WC2E 7HF

(Animals) *Royal Society for Prevention of Cruelty to Animals*, The Causeway, Horsham, Sussex RH12 1HG
World Wildlife Fund, Education Dept, 11-13 Ockford Rd, Godalming, Surrey GU7 1QU

(Blind) *Royal Commonwealth Society for the Blind,* Commonwealth House, Haywards Heath, West Sussex
Royal National Institute for the Blind, 224 Great Portland St, London W1N 6AA

Central Rescue Station, 7 South Parade, Doncaster, S Yorks

Christian Aid Secondary Education Advisor, PO Box No 1, London SW9 8BH

(Coal) *National Coal Board,* Hobart House, Grosvenor Place, London SW1X 7AE

Customs and Excise (Board of) King's Beam House, Mark Lane, London EC3

(Deaf) *Royal National Institute for the Deaf,* 105 Gower St, London WC1

Fair trading, Office of, Field House, Bream's Buildings, London EC4

Health Education Council, 78 New Oxford St, London WC1 1AH

Her Majesty's Stationery Office, Atlantic House, Holborn Viaduct, London EC1

(Interfaith) *Wolverhampton Interfaith Group,* 2 Church St, Wolverhampton, W Midlands
Shap Working Party, 7 Alderbrook Rd, Solihull, W Midlands B91 1NH

(Lifeboats) *Royal National Lifeboat Institution,* West Quay Rd, Poole, Dorset BH15 1HZ

Oxfam, 274 Banbury Rd, Oxford OX2 7DZ

Postal Museum (National), King Edward St, London EC1A 1LP

Racial Equality, Commission for, Elliot House, 10-12 Allington St, London SW1

Red Cross Society, 9 Grosvenor Cres, London SW1X 7EJ

Samaritans, 17 Uxbridge Rd, Slough

Sikh Educational and Cultural Society, Sat-Nam Cottage, Compton Gardens, Kinver, W Midlands

(Social Security) *Department of Health and Social Security*, Alexander Fleming House, Elephant & Castle, London SE1 6BY

(Water) *National Water Council*, 1 Queen Anne's Gate, London SW1H 9BT

Subject Index

The name of the Assembly is given in brackets. The number indicates the chapter number in this book.

A Word for Your Year

Assembly Checklist

Date	Group	Subject used	Initials

Assembly Checklist

Date	Group	Subject used	Initials

Date	Group	Subject used	Initials

Assembly Checklist

Date	Group	Subject used	Initials